AIR CAMPAIGN

HOLLAND 1940

The Luftwaffe's first setback in the West

T0323356

RYAN K. NOPPEN | ILLUSTRATED BY ADAM TOOBY

OSPREY PUBLISHING
Bloomsbury Publishing Plc
Kemp House, Chawley Park, Cumnor Hill, Oxford OX2 9PH, UK
29 Earlsfort Terrace, Dublin 2, Ireland
1385 Broadway, 5th Floor, New York, NY 10018, USA
E-mail: info@ospreypublishing.com
www.ospreypublishing.com

OSPREY is a trademark of Osprey Publishing Ltd

First published in Great Britain in 2021

A catalogue record for this book is available from the British Library.

ISBN: PB 9781472846686; eBook 9781472846693;
ePDF 9781472846662; XML 9781472846679

22 23 24 25   10 9 8 7 6 5 4 3 2

Maps by www.bounford.com
Diagrams by Adam Tooby
3D BEVs by Paul Kime
Index by Alison Worthington
Typeset by PDQ Digital Media Solutions, Bungay, UK
Printed and bound in India by Replika Press Private Ltd.

Author's Acknowledgements
The author wishes to thank Douglas
Dildy for his research assistance and
lengthy discussions over this project.
The author also wishes to thank his
lovely wife Sarah and his beautiful little
peanut Emma for allowing him the time
to write this work.

Reference Guide
Militaire Luchtvaart Organization
Afdeeling (or squadron) – one squadron
Groep (or group) – four squadrons
(intended)
Luchtvaartregiment (aviation regiment) –
a Jachtgroep and another Groep
**Militaire Luchtvaart Terms and
Abbreviations**
Bombardeervliegtuigafdeeling (BomVA),
or bomber squadron
Commando Luchtverdediging (C.-Lvd.),
or air defence command
Jachtvliegtuigafdeeling (JaVA), or fighter
squadron
Strategische Verkenningsvliegtuig Afdeling
(StratVerVA), or strategic reconnaissance
squadron
Verkenningsgroep (Verk.Gr.), or
reconnaissance/observation squadron
Luftwaffe Organization
Rotte – two fighters (leader and wing-
man); basic Luftwaffe fighter tactical
combat unit
Kette – three bombers; basic Luftwaffe
bomber tactical combat unit
Schwarm – two Rotten of fighters
Staffel – three Schwärme or Ketten
Gruppe – three Staffeln
Geschwader – three to four Gruppen
Fliegerkorps – several Geschwader; basic
Luftwaffe operational combat unit
Luftflotte – one or more Fliegerkorps
Luftwaffe Abbreviations and Terms
JG – *Jagdgeschwader*, or fighter wing
ZG - *Zerstörergeschwader*, or heavy
fighter wing
KG – *Kampfgeschwader*, or bomber wing
StG – *Sturzkampfgeschwader*, or dive-
bomber wing
LG – *Lehrgeschwader*, or experimental/
instructional wing
Aufkl.Gr. – *Aufklärungsgruppe*, or
reconnaissance group

AIR CAMPAIGN

CONTENTS

INTRODUCTION

On 27 September 1939, the day after the conclusion of the German campaign in Poland, Adolf Hitler called together the *Oberkommando der Wehrmacht* (Supreme Command of the Armed Forces), or OKW, and chiefs of the *Heer, Kriegsmarine*, and *Luftwaffe*, and ordered them to prepare plans for *Fall Gelb* (Case Yellow), an offensive move against the British and French armies in Western Europe. Hitler did not want to fight a long war against the Western Allies and believed that their forces would only grow stronger as time marched on; citing the vulnerability of Germany's industrial Rühr region to a potential Allied offensive once their forces were organized, Hitler insisted on immediate offensive action in order to maintain German initiative in the conflict. The *Oberkommando des Heeres* (Army High Command), or OKH, drafted *Aufmarschanweisung N°1, Fall Gelb* (Deployment Plan No. 1, Case Yellow) for a westward sweep across the Netherlands, Belgium, and Luxembourg, bypassing the Maginot Line but pitting German forces into a frontal attack against Allied forces in northern France. German ground forces in the west were divided into three army groups: *Heeresgruppe B* in the north (positioned against the Netherlands and northern Belgium), *Heeresgruppe A* in the centre (positioned against central and southern Belgium), and *Heeresgruppe C* in the south (covering Heeresgruppe A's flank and the southwestern German border).

Hitler had no qualms about violating Belgian neutrality, arguing that the small nation was involved in active defence negotiations with the French, but questioned the strategic practicality of moving through Dutch territory. He insisted upon a revision to the original OKH plan, authorizing German movement through the Maastricht Strip, a narrow strip of Dutch territory running north-to-south along the River Maas for roughly 50km along the Belgian eastern border down to the city of Maastricht, but with a political arrangement to be worked out with the Dutch government; Dutch territory was not to be occupied and Dutch neutrality was to be maintained. Halder unveiled the amended Aufmarschanweisung N°2, Fall Gelb, which excluded the occupation of Dutch territory on 29 October 1939.

Oberbefehlshaber der Luftwaffe (Luftwaffe supreme commander) Hermann Göring and *Chef des Generalstabs der Luftwaffe* (Luftwaffe chief-of-staff) *Generalmajor* Hans Jeschonnek were immediately alarmed at the omission of the Netherlands from the territory to be occupied in the revised plan for Fall Gelb, fearing that the British would not hesitate to violate Dutch neutrality in order for the Royal Air Force to make use of Dutch airfields for attacks on targets in the Rühr. Jeschonnek went to see Hitler on 30 October and unsuccessfully tried to convince him to again make the Netherlands a target of Fall Gelb.

Hitler hoped to launch Fall Gelb on 12 November but poor weather compelled its postponement (Fall Gelb would ultimately be postponed 20 times for various reasons between 12 November 1939 and 10 May 1940); this postponement allowed Jeschonnek more time to plead his case for the Netherlands to Hitler. The threat of British use of Dutch airfields as well as Jeschonnek's additional argument that the Dutch themselves were not fully capable of preventing British overflights of Dutch territory en route to targets in the Rühr finally persuaded Hitler to again earmark Dutch territory for occupation.

On 15 November at Hitler's prompting, OKW issued new instructions that the occupation of as much Dutch territory as possible for the purpose of securing the air defence of the Rühr was now a priority for the army in Fall Gelb. OKH felt at the time it could only spare the X.Armeekorps (at the time two infantry divisions and the army's sole cavalry division) from the 18.Armee, the force responsible for covering the German northern flank in the West, and several armoured trains for operations against the Netherlands; OKH concluded that these units could occupy Dutch territory leading up to the *Grebbelinie* (Grebbe Line) in the central Netherlands and territory south of the River Maas; this excluded the area of the Netherlands referred to as *Vesting Holland* (Fortress Holland).

Generalmajor Hans Jeschonnek (right), the Luftwaffe's chief-of-staff, was the primary proponent of the complete occupation of the Netherlands as the German high command planned its invasion of the West. Jeschonnek convinced his superior, Hermann Göring (left), that German control of Dutch airfields had to be immediately accomplished at the outset of the offensive or risk the threat of the British Royal Air Force occupying them and using them for raids against the Rühr industrial basin. (Getty Images)

The Dutch defences

It is necessary at this point to briefly discuss the Dutch defensive positions and geographical barriers facing German army planners at the time. The Grebbelinie was a modern defence line, made up of trenches and concrete bunkers, running north-to-south from the Ijsselmeer to just east of the town of Rhenen on the Rhine River and then southward to Ochten on the Waal River and ending near Appeltern on the Maas. To the south beginning at the town of Grave on the Maas was the *Peel-Raamstelling* (Peel-Raam Position), a lighter defence line of pillboxes, barbed wire, and peat marshes running south and west to the Belgian border near the town of Weert.

To the west of the Grebbeline was the *Waterlinie* (Waterline), running north-to-south from the Ijsselmeer through Utrecht and across the Rhine, Waal, and Maas. The Waterline, the traditional defensive line protecting the provinces of Holland and Zeeland since the Golden Age of the seventeenth century, ran along the easternmost part of the country below sea level and was composed of fields that could be flooded with several feet of water – just enough to prevent the advance of armies marching on foot. In the late 1930s modern pillboxes were added along the line.

The Waterlinie was the eastern boundary of the Vesting Holland, the area north of the Waal and Maas estuaries that encompassed the urban centres of Amsterdam, Rotterdam, Den Haag, and Utrecht; it was considered the national redoubt of the country. If the Waterlinie was flooded, the only route of approach into the Vesting Holland were the road and rail bridges over the Hollands Diep at Moerdijk, the Oude Maas at Dordrecht, and the Nieuwe Maas at Rotterdam. The primary southern defensive boundaries of the Grebbelinie, Waterlinie, and Vesting Holland were the east-to-west flowing tributaries of the Rhine, Waal, and Maas.

Jeschonnek immediately made it known he was not satisfied with the 'halfway' occupation initially proposed by OKH as all but one of the major airfields in the Netherlands were located inside of the Vesting Holland – still leaving them open to potential British use. Generaloberst Fedor von Bock, commander of Heeresgruppe B, was also displeased with the plan not to occupy the Vesting Holland; he was uncomfortable with the idea of leaving open a potential staging ground for Allied forces which could threaten his flank and rear. The question of the partial- versus full- occupation of the Netherlands was not resolved until mid-January 1940 in the wake of the Mechelen Incident, in which the plans for the Aufmarschanweisung N°2 variant of Fall Gelb fell into Belgian hands when a Luftwaffe aircraft accidentally landed in Belgian territory in heavy fog.

As part of the now necessary revisions applied to Fall Gelb, on 14 January Hitler finally agreed with Jeschonnek and Bock that the Netherlands should be completely occupied, albeit quickly so as not to deter from the main push through Belgium and northern France. Bock concurred on the rapid conquest, wanting to secure his flank quickly, and assigned the entire 18.Armee to the task. The most potent unit in 18.Armee was the 9.Panzer-Division, recently formed in January 1940 from elements originating in the Austrian *Bundesheer*'s mobile *Schnelle Division*. On 10 May 1940, the 9.Panzer-Division possessed the following tanks and armoured vehicles: 30× PzKpfw I, 54× PzKpfw II, 41× PzKpfw III, 16× PzKpfw IV, 12× PzBfWg IV (*Panzerbefehlwagen* or 'command tank'), and 62× armoured cars; around half of these tanks came from the *Panzer-Lehr-Abteilung*, or Panzer training unit. Although understrength, the mission of the 9.Panzer-Division was to surge through a breach in the Grebbelinie/Peel-Raamstelling, race westwards parallel to the Maas, and then assault the Vesting Holland from the south, travelling up the motorway between Moerdijk and Rotterdam.

Fallschirmjäger and Luftlande troops

In order for the 9.Panzer-Division to enter the Vesting Holland quickly, the road bridges over the waterways of the Hollands Diep at Moerdijk, the Oude Maas at Dordrecht, and the Nieuwe Maas at Rotterdam had to be captured intact. On 11 January 1940, OKW enquired whether the *Fallschirmjäger* (airborne) units of the Luftwaffe could be used to secure these bridges and other key points within the Vesting Holland and hold them until the arrival of the 9.Panzer-Division. Initially OKH suggested that Fallschirmjäger units be dropped behind the Grebbelinie and assist army ground units with breaching it.

Generalleutnant Kurt Student, a World War I fighter pilot and commander of the Luftwaffe's 7.Fliegerdivision, dismissed OKH's proposed Grebbelinie operation as too limited in strategic value and countered with a much bolder proposal: using the paratroopers of his 7.Fliegerdivision and the troops of the 22.Luftlande-Division or 'air-landing division' (an infantry division trained to be deployed via transport aircraft) to secure not only the vital bridges at Moerdijk, Dordrecht, and Rotterdam but to seize other vital targets, such as Dutch airfields, within the Vesting Holland as well. If Dutch airfields could be secured by

Fallschirmjäger paratroopers, Luftlande troopers could be landed on and supplied via them by transport aircraft; this would allow for a sizeable force to operate well behind enemy lines and assist with the main effort to breach the Vesting Holland. This was something of a revolutionary proposal as airborne forces, experimented with by several nations during the interwar years, had never been deployed in combat, let alone in strength.

Originally Fallschirmjäger units were intended to serve in a commando role, landing behind enemy lines to capture or destroy key logistical targets such as bridges, airfields, crossroads, and supply depots. Student believed that Fallschirmjäger, deployed in force, could fulfil more than just unconventional tactical roles. Since taking command of all of the Luftwaffe's airborne units in July 1938, Student incorporated light artillery, anti-tank, reconnaissance, and other specialized units into his force that could be dropped or landed alongside his paratroopers, with the intention that they could be deployed as a highly mobile light division capable of operating independently in the enemy's rear. By the beginning of 1940, Student's 4,500-man 7.Fliegerdivision consisted of two regiments, made of up of 2–3 battalions, each containing three rifle companies and one machine-gun company. The Fallschirmjäger of the 7.Fliegerdivision would be supported by the 12,000-man 22.Luftlande-Division. The Luftwaffe realized the potential of using aircraft for the rapid movement and deployment of troops at the beginning of the Spanish Civil War when it carried out the transport, with Junkers Ju 52/3m airliners commandeered from Deutsche Lufthansa, of over 13,500 Nationalist troops and nearly 300 tons of weapons and supplies from Morocco to Spain in the late summer of 1936. In October 1939, OKW decided to convert the 22.Infanterie-Division into a Luftlande-Division and its units were put through rapid deployment exercises.

Student was confident that these elite units could perform such strategic objectives; he further emphasized that such an operation could meet the strategic needs of both the army (capture of bridges) and Luftwaffe (capture of airfields). Student presented his proposal to Jeschonnek and Generalmajor Alfred Jodl, *Chef des Wehrmachtführungsstabes* (Chief of Operation Staff) for OKW, who were both enthusiastic about the potential returns for the commitment of a relatively small number of forces and in turn presented the plan to Hitler. *Der Führer* was fascinated with the offensive potential, vis-a-vis other Blitzkrieg tactics, offered by airborne operations.

On 14 January 1940, Hitler approved the proposal for *Unternehmen F* (*Festung*, or fortress) and insisted that it achieve: 1. The capture of the bridges at Moerdijk, Dordrecht, and Rotterdam in order to secure the advance of the 18.Armee into the Vesting Holland and; 2. The rapid occupation of the Dutch capital, Den Haag, and capture of the Dutch military and political leadership. This second objective came from an idea, largely from the commander of the 22.Luftlande-Division Generalleutnant Hans Graf von Sponeck, that the Dutch leadership might be convinced to peacefully accept German military 'protection' if the attack on the Netherlands was called off at the outset. Kurt Student was to command the Luftlandekorps, created *an der Kommandoweg aufgestellt* or 'provisionally', made up of the 4,500-man 7.Fliegerdivision and the 12,000-man 22.Luftlande-Division for the duration of Fall Gelb.

Fallschirmjäger recruits making a practice jump near the Luftwaffe's paratrooper training school at Stendal in 1938. Student instilled a fierce *esprit de corps* among his officers and troopers and placed special emphasis upon *Auftragstaktik*, or mission tactics, during their training. Independent initiative was encouraged to aggressively accomplish the mission objective by whatever means necessary. (Getty Images)

The road and rail bridges over the Hollands Diep waterway at Moerdijk were the southern gateways in the Vesting Holland and had to be captured intact by General Student's Fallschirmjäger if the tanks of the 9.Panzer-Division were to breach the Dutch Waterlinie. (Collectie Nederlands Instituut voor Militaire Historie)

OKW intended Unternehmen F to be a *Strategischer Überfall* or 'strategic assault' with a strategic objective: the rapid capitulation and occupation of the entire Netherlands within a matter of days, thus quickly securing the northern flank of Heeresgruppe B and allowing it to conduct its primary operations without the threat of Allied ground interference with its flank or rear. Jeschonnek saw it as the means to achieve a Luftwaffe strategic objective: to secure Dutch airfields from potential Allied use; an added bonus would be to demonstrate the versatility of the Luftwaffe as an independent arm of the Wehrmacht (particularly in light of the intense interservice rivalry among the branches of the Wehrmacht) as Unternehmen F would be solely a Luftwaffe operation – until the panzers of 9.Panzer-Division arrived to relieve the airborne units.

Generaloberst von Bock was initially sceptical about the importance or chance of success of the Luftlande operation at Den Haag but recognized the value of the Moerdijk-Dordrecht-Rotterdam bridges being secured; in his mind it would be the 18.Armee, and specifically the 9.Panzer-Division, that ensured the defeat of the Netherlands and he believed that the airborne operations were merely tactical measures for this larger army operation. Bock instructed the commander of the 18.Armee, General der Artillerie Georg von Küchler, that he had three days to breach the Vesting Holland from the south after the first day of the airborne operation and bring about a Dutch capitulation. Regardless of what various commanders expected from Unternehmen F, it was a significant undertaking as it would be the first mass airborne operation in the history of warfare.

ATTACKER'S CAPABILITIES
Luftflotte 2 in the Holland operation

As mentioned previously, Unternehmen F was to be an independent Luftwaffe undertaking until ground elements of the 18.Armee arrived to relieve the airborne units and assume occupation of captured Dutch territory. As such it fell under the jurisdiction of the air fleet based in north-west Germany and assigned to support the operations of Heeresgruppe B in the Netherlands and Belgium: Luftflotte 2, commanded by General der Flieger Albert Kesselring.

Having served as Chef des Generalstabs der Luftwaffe in 1936–37 and commander of Luftflotte 1 during the Polish Campaign, Kesselring was a veteran air fleet commander who had helped to develop the Luftwaffe's combat aircraft and offensive tactics, as well as the first Fallschirmjäger units. As demonstrated in Poland, he particularly understood the importance of immediate attacks on enemy airfields and aviation infrastructure as the means to achieving air superiority at the outset of a campaign. Unternehmen F was just one mission among several expected to be carried out by Luftflotte 2 at the outset of Fall Gelb however. Only two air fleets were assigned to Fall Gelb: Kesselring's Luftflotte 2 and Luftflotte 3, led by General der Flieger Hugo Sperrle, which was tasked with covering the operations of Heeresgruppen A and C. By late February 1940, OKW had revised Fall Gelb yet again based upon proposals by Generalleutnant Erich von Manstein, Chef des Generalstabs der Heeresgruppe A: the *Aufmarschanweisung N°4* variant called for the *Schwerpunkt* (main area of execution) of Fall Gelb to be a concentrated push through the Ardennes towards Sedan and was assigned to Heeresgruppe A, which was reinforced at the expense of Heeresgruppe B.

After the adoption of Aufmarschanweisung N°4 Fall Gelb, Heeresgruppe B consisted of 6.Armee and the previously discussed 18.Armee. As a result of the strengthening of Heeresgruppe B, Luftflotte 3, assigned to cover the operations of Heeresgruppe A and C, was given considerably more aircraft than Luftflotte 2. Nonetheless Kesselring's squadrons were expected to support the airborne operations in the Netherlands, the ground assaults in the Netherlands and northern Belgium, and simultaneously provide air defence for the urban and industrial areas of the Ruhr. Of the five larger units which composed Luftflotte 2,

By the beginning of Fall Gelb, the majority of the Luftwaffe's single-engine fighter squadrons had been re-equipped with the E variant of the Messerschmitt Bf 109. It was the most numerous of the German fighters to see action during Unternehmen F. This Bf 109E03, with markings for JG 51 and camouflage which would have been used in the spring of 1940, is housed in the Deutsches Museum in Munich. (Arjun Sarup/ CC-BY-SA-4.0)

General der Flieger Albert Kesselring, commander of Luftflotte 2, speaking with pilots of Zerstörergeschwader 26. (Getty Images)

Kesselring assigned VIII.Fliegerkorps and most of IV.Fliegerkorps to support 6.Armee's drive across northern Belgium as well as the airborne operation against Eben-Emael.

Two of Luftflotte 2's larger units were specifically designated for Unternehmen F. Fliegerkorps zbV.2 (Fliegerkorps zur besonderen Verwendung 2 or 'air corps for special deployment') was a mixed unit of He 111H/P, Ju 88A bombers and Ju 87B dive-bombers, which was assembled specifically to provide close support for the airborne and air-landing operations in the Netherlands. The Luftlandekorps, consisting of 460 Junkers Ju 52/3m transports and several other reconnaissance and support aircraft, was responsible for airborne and air-landing operations. Luftflotte 2's final larger unit was Jagdfliegerführer 2's, whose fighters would provide cover for Heeresgruppe B's entire front. If needed, Kesselring could also call on the Bf 109D/E fighters of the Jagdfliegerführer Deutsche Bucht, based on airfields in northern Germany, for missions over the northern Netherlands (*see pg. 15 for Luftflotte 2's full order of battle*).

Fighter cover for airborne operations

For an operation involving such a large number of transport aircraft, the cover provided by Jagdfliegerführer 2's Bf 109s and Bf 110s would be essential for the success of the airborne and air-landing missions. Kesselring intended to use rotating flights of Jagdfliegerführer 2's fighters as a continuous umbrella to provide cover for the airborne and airlanding target areas in the Vesting Holland. This was to protect the movement of the highly vulnerable Ju 52/3m transports carrying Luftlande units as well as defend the exposed Fallschirmjäger units from attacks by Dutch aircraft or interloping British or French aircraft.

With a maximum speed of 354mph and an armament of two 7.92mm MG 17 machine guns mounted in the engine cowl and two wing-mounted 20mm MG FF/M cannon, the Messerschmitt Bf 109E had proved to be a formidable fighter in the skies over Poland and at the outset of Fall Gelb, the Luftwaffe's Bf 109 pilots had high morale and exuded a great deal of confidence. Unternehmen F would expose a serious limitation in the operational capabilities of the Bf 109 however. The Bf 109E only had a normal range of 412 miles and an effective combat radius of roughly 180 miles due to the high-power output of the DB601 engine, resulting in fuel being consumed at a high rate. This was not considered to be a problem during the fighter's development as the aircraft was designed as a high-speed interceptor. Extended combat air patrol by Bf 109s had only previously been flown just ahead of moving ground columns in Poland with the objective of clearing the skies of enemy aircraft. Bf 109s also provided escort for close air support missions primarily flown by Ju 87s, which themselves had a maximum range of 370 miles.

Messerschmitt Bf 109E-3	
Length:	28ft 4in (8.6m)
Wingspan:	32ft 6.5in (9.9m)
Powerplant:	1,100hp Daimler-Benz DB 601A-1 inline engine
Maximum speed:	354mph (570km/h)
Range:	412 miles (663km)
Ceiling:	37,731ft (11,500m)
Armament:	2 x 7.92mm MG 17 machine guns, 2 x 20mm MG FF cannons

The Luftwaffe was aware of the range limitations of the Bf 109s and Stukas for these missions but remedied the situation through the use of mobile logistics units which could set up and maintain forward airfields near the front lines as well as quickly repairing and readying captured enemy airfields for German use. As Jagdfliegerführer 2's Bf 109s were to provide cover for ground forces landing and operating behind enemy lines, the use of Luftwaffe mobile logistics units to operate forward airfields was not possible in Unternehmen F – not until army ground forces secured the captured territory and established a line of supply.

Jagdfliegerführer 2's fighters, operating from airfields around the Dortmund-Essen area had an average distance of 90–100 miles to fly before reaching their patrol areas over the Vesting Holland; this allowed for 10–20 minutes of flight time over their patrol area depending upon the rate of fuel consumption if required to engage in combat. This shortcoming apparently did not overly worry Generalmajor Kurt-Bertram von Döring, commander of Jagdfliegerführer 2, since he drafted a timetable which on paper made it appear that his units could maintain a continuous fighter umbrella. Nevertheless, he underestimated the rapid fuel consumption of the Bf 109 as well as the actual area his fighters were required to cover – roughly 1,800 square miles.

Another reason why Döring may not have concerned himself with the limited range of his Bf 109 fighters was that he had four Zerstörergruppen of Messerschmitt Bf 110C/D twin-engine heavy fighters available for extended combat air patrol duty. First flown in May 1936, the Bf 110 *Zerstörer* (destroyer) was intended to serve as a long-range escort fighter. At the time, designers reasoned that long range could only be achieved in a fighter that was larger and could thus accommodate larger fuel tanks; the larger size and greater weight however made this aircraft less manoeuvrable than single-engine fighters. To make up for this shortcoming two powerful engines were installed to give the aircraft enough speed to evade single-engine fighters as well as a heavy armament which could down enemy aircraft with only a short burst.

Messerschmitt Bf 110C-4	
Length:	39ft 8.5in (12.1m)
Wingspan:	53ft 5in (16.2m)
Powerplant:	2 x 1,100hp Daimler-Benz DB 601B-1 inline engines
Maximum speed:	349mph (560km/h)
Range:	565 miles (910km)
Ceiling:	32,811ft (10,000m)
Armament:	4 x 7.92mm MG 17 machine guns, 2 x 20mm MG FF/M cannons, 1 x 7.92mm MG 15 machine gun for defence
Crew:	2

The pilots of the Luftwaffe's Zerstörergeschwader achieved a number of kills, destroyed numerous aircraft on the ground, and sustained minimal losses during Unternehmen F. Misinterpreting the results of the Netherlands campaign, Luftwaffe planners overestimated the capabilities of the new Messerschmitt Bf 110 heavy fighter and, as a result, the aircraft and its pilots would suffer heavy losses against high-performance single-engine fighters in the Battle of Britain. This surviving Bf 110F-2 is housed in the Deutsches Technikmuseum in Berlin. (Author's collection)

Beginning in February 1939 the Luftwaffe began to take delivery of the Bf 110C variant, powered by two DB601 engines which gave the aircraft a maximum speed of 349mph – only slightly slower than the Bf 109. Armament consisted of four MG 17 machine guns and two MG FF/M cannon in the nose. Göring was so confident about the capabilities of the Bf 110 that in late 1938 he formed specific Zerstörergeschwader and transferred a number of the Luftwaffe's best fighter pilots to them.

The long-range escort missions which Zerstörergeschwader pilots were trained to perform were not intended to be close escort; rather the Bf 110s were to fly ahead of the bombers and clear the skies over the target area using dive-and-climb combat tactics, making maximum use of the aircraft's speed and armament. Bf 110 pilots put these tactics to great use over Poland and the Zerstörer units shot down 54 Polish aircraft for a loss of only seven Bf 110s in combat. Bf 110s also saw success in the skies over Denmark and Norway during *Unternehmen Weserübung*, the German invasion of those countries on 9 April 1940, destroying most of their opposition on the ground during strafing runs; these actions seemed to prove to many Bf 110 pilots, and the Luftwaffe's leadership, that the Bf 110 was perfectly suited to the long-range escort role as well as seeming to vindicate the theory that twin-engine heavy fighters could effectively duel with single-engine fighters.

Some Zerstörer pilots noted that the Bf 110 suffered from very poor manoeuvrability however, and there were several losses in Poland and Norway to outmoded but highly manoeuvrable PZL P.11 parasol monoplanes and Gloster Gladiator biplanes. These concerns largely fell on deaf ears nevertheless due to the overall success experienced by the Zerstörer units as well as the perceptions of invincibility being fostered by the Luftwaffe high command. Within this context, Döring was confident that Bf 109s and Bf 110s, operating in concert, would provide sufficient cover for both longer-range bombing missions and the air-landing operations in the Netherlands.

Strike capabilities

Bombardment operations in support of Unternehmen F were to be carried out by Fliegerkorps zbV.2, led by Generalmajor Richard Putzier. As this unit was specially organized solely for the support of the airborne and air-landing missions in the Vesting Holland, the decision of

which targets to strike and its coordination with Fallschirmjäger and Luftlande forces on the ground was left up to Putzier. He realized that effective support of these missions required the ability to suppress aerial opposition by destroying enemy aircraft on the ground as well as disabling enemy airfields; it also called for the ability to attack individual targets, such as anti-aircraft and artillery batteries, defensive hardpoints, machine-gun positions, and enemy columns and vehicles with a high degree of precision.

To that end Putzier had three different types of bombers which each could perform such specialized tasks. The most numerous aircraft within Fliegerkorps zbV.2 was the Heinkel He 111 medium bomber. Its maximum payload of 4,410lb was comparable to most other medium bombers being developed by other nations and was not seen as light until the entry into service of American and British heavy bombers later in World War II. The Luftwaffe high command viewed the He 111 as a 'long-range' bomber and deployed it against targets in Poland beyond the range of its Stukas. He 111s would be deployed in the 'long-range' role by Putzier over the Netherlands and would be covered by Bf 110s from Jagdfliegerführer 2's fighter umbrella.

The Heinkel He 111P was the most numerous Luftwaffe bomber assigned to Unternehmen F. This surviving He 111P is housed in the Forsvarets Flysamling Gardermoen museum near Oslo. (Aeroprints.com/CC-BY-SA-3.0)

Heinkel He 111P	
Length:	53ft 9½in (16.4m)
Wingspan:	74ft 2in (22.6m)
Powerplant:	2 x 1,100hp Daimler-Benz DB 601A-1 inline engines
Maximum speed:	242mph (390km/h)
Range:	745 miles (1,200km)
Ceiling:	25,590ft (7,800m)
Armament:	3 x 7.92mm MG 15 machine guns
Payload:	4,410lb (2000kg) of bombs
Crew:	5

For precision attacks, Putzier was assigned a Gruppe of Junkers Ju 87 Stukas (abbreviated from *Sturzkampfflugzeug* or dive-bomber) from Lehrgeschwader 1, a Luftwaffe training unit which tested new equipment and tactics and which was equipped with both fighters and bombers. By the end of the Polish Campaign, the use of Ju 87s as airborne artillery, flying

in advance of the panzers, had become a refined tactic of the Wehrmacht and became the most visible image of the Blitzkrieg theory. As such, most of the Ju 87 units within Luftflotte 2 were earmarked for close support missions for the 6. and 18.Armee. IV.(St.)/LG1 however was tasked with supporting the Fallschirmjäger of the 7.Fliegerdivision, specifically for precision strikes against defensive hardpoints located around the paratroopers' objectives. As IV.(St.)/LG1 was the only Stukagruppe assigned to Unternehmen F, its capability for precision strikes had to be used judiciously.

With its ability to serve as both a horizontal bomber and dive-bomber as well as its relatively high speed, the new Junkers Ju 88s assigned to Unternehmen F were highly prized by General Putzier and extensively used throughout the campaign. Their frequent use led to high losses however. This Ju 88D-1 is preserved in the National Museum of the United States Air Force in Dayton, Ohio. (Author's collection)

The most versatile bomber Putzier had at his disposal was the Junkers Ju 88 but, as with the Ju 87, he only had a limited number: 21 Ju 88A-1s within III./KG4. The Ju 88A-1 was a reasonably fast aircraft which could perform horizontal and dive-bombing missions, with a payload of up to 6,600lb and a maximum range of 1,696 miles. Efforts to make the aircraft an effective dive-bomber slowed its development and its introduction into service was further delayed as its high-performance characteristics made it a more difficult aircraft to fly and bomber pilots switching to the type required extensive training. The Ju 88's range particularly made the aircraft a valuable asset for operations over the Vesting Holland but, as with the Ju 87s, the small number available meant that their deployment would have to be prioritized.

Junkers Ju 88A-1	
Length:	47ft 3in (14.4m)
Wingspan:	65ft 7.5in (20m)
Powerplant:	2 x 1,200hp Jumo 211B-1 inline engines
Maximum speed:	292mph (470km/h)
Range:	1,696 miles (2,730km)
Ceiling:	26,900ft (8,200m)
Armament:	3 x 7.92mm MG 15 machine guns
Payload:	4,189lbs (1,900kg) of bombs
Crew:	4

The transports

The final aircraft earmarked for extensive service in Unternehmen F was the Junkers Ju 52/3m/ transport, which made up the majority of the aircraft in Student's Luftlandekorps. By the time of the Polish Campaign, 99 per cent of the Luftwaffe's transport and lift capacity was made up of Ju 52/3ms. When used in Fallschirmjäger operations, a Ju 52/3m typically carried a squad (12 paratroopers) and its weapons. When assigned to air-landing missions, Ju 52/3m could carry 16–18 lightly armed troops aboard but, prior to Unternehmen F, the number of troops per aircraft was reduced to 9–10 so that each soldier had his full armament with him – a better tactical situation if they had to engage in combat immediately upon exiting the aircraft.

The Achilles heel of the Ju 52/3m in a combat situation, particularly airborne and air-landing missions, was the fact that it was an older airliner design; its maximum speed was only 168mph and had no dedicated defensive protection. Air superiority was thus deemed an essential prerequisite to the success of the airborne and air-landing missions in the Vesting Holland. Furthermore, the Luftwaffe could ill-afford to lose many of its transports; almost all were assigned to missions at the beginning of Fall Gelb, with 412 alone earmarked for Unternehmen F. It is worth noting that the Luftwaffe had already lost a substantial number of Ju 52/3ms in the Norway Campaign prior to Fall Gelb, total losses coming to roughly 25 per cent of its transport force by the end of the campaign in June 1940.

The Junkers Ju 52/3m transport, first flown in 1932, was the most common Luftwaffe transport throughout World War II. It could accommodate 12 Fallschirmjäger or up to 18 lightly-armed Luftlande troops. This German-built Ju 52/3mg4e is preserved in the Forsvarets Flysamling Gardermoen museum near Oslo. (Clemens Vasters/CC-BY-2.0)

Junkers Ju 52/3m	
Length:	62ft (18.9m)
Wingspan:	95ft 11½in (29.25m)
Powerplant:	3 x 715hp BMW 132T radial engines
Maximum speed:	168mph (270km/h)
Range:	795 miles (1,280 km)
Armament:	1-3 7.92mm MG 15 machine guns
Crew:	2

ORDER OF BATTLE – 10 MAY 1940

Luftwaffe Units Assigned to Unternehmen F
Luftflotte 2 (Münster) – General der Flieger Albert Kesselring
Jagdfliegerführer 2 (Dortmund) – Generalmajor Kurt-Bertram von Döring
Jagdgeschwader 1
Stab IV.(N)/JG 2 (Hopsten) – Hauptmann Albert Blumensaat (*3× Bf 109D*)
10.(N)/JG 2 (Hopsten) – Oberleutnant Erwin Bacsila (*10× Bf 109D*)
2./ZG 76 (Köln-Wahn) – Oberleutnant Gustav Uellenbeck (*10× Bf 110C/D*)

II.(J)/Tr.Gr. 186 (Wangerooge) – Hauptmann Anton Seeliger (*35× Bf 109E*)
Jagdgeschwader 26
Stab JG 26 (Dortmund) – Major Hans-Hugo Witt (*3× Bf 109E*)
II./JG 26 (Dortmund) – Hauptmann Herwig Knüppel (*36× Bf 109E*)
III./JG 26 (Essen-Mülheim) – Major Ernst Freiherr von Berg (*22× Bf 109E*)
III./JG 3 (Hopsten) – Hauptmann Walter Kienitz (*25× Bf 109E*)

Jagdgeschwader 51

Stab JG 51 (Bönninghardt) – Oberst Theo Osterkamp
(3× Bf 109E)

I./JG 20 (Bönninghardt) – Hauptmann Hannes Trautloft
(36× Bf 109E)

I./JG 26 (Bönninghardt) – Major Gotthardt Handrick
(35× Bf 109E)

I./JG 51 (Krefeld) – Hauptmann Hans-Heinrich Brustellin
(38× Bf 109E)

II./JG 27 (Wesel) – Hauptmann Walter Andres
(23× Bf 109E)

Zerstörergeschwader 26

Stab ZG 26 (Dortmund) – Oberstleutnant Joachim-
Friedrich Huth (3× Bf 110C)

I./ZG 1 (Kirchhellen) – Hauptmann Wolfgang Falck
(22× Bf 110C/D)

II./ZG 1 (Gelsenkirchen-Buer) – Hauptmann Friedrich-
Karl Dickoré (26× Bf 110C)

2./ZG 76 (Aalborg) – Oberleutnant Gustav Uellenbeck
(12× Bf 110C)

Fliegerkorps zur besonderen Verwendung 2 (Bremen) – Generalmajor Richard Putzier

Kampfgeschwader 4

Stab KG 4 (Fassberg) – Oberst Martin Fiebig
(6× He 111P)

I./KG 4 (Gütersloh) – Oberstleutnant Hans-Joachim Rath
(24× He 111H)

II./KG 4 (Fassberg) – Major Dietrich Freiherr von
Massenbach (18× He 111P)

III./KG 4 (Delmenhorst) – Hauptmann Erich Blödorn
(11× He 111P; 21× Ju 88)

IV.(Stuka)/Lehrgeschwader 1 (Duisburg) – Hauptmann
Peter Kögl (37× Ju 87B)

Aufklärungsstaffel zbV.2 (Bremen) – Oberleutnant
Herbert Sewing (4× Do 17M; 1× He 111H)

IV.Fliegerkorps (Düsseldorf) – General der Flieger Alfred Keller

Kampfgeschwader 30

Stab KG 30 (Oldenburg) – Oberleutnant Walter Loebel
(2× Ju 88A)

I./KG 30 (Oldenburg) – Hauptmann Fritz Doench
(25× Ju 88A)

II./KG 30 (Oldenburg) – Hauptmann Claus Hinkelbein
(25× Ju 88A)

7.Fliegerdivision (Köln) – Generalleutnant Kurt Student

Kampfgeschwader zur besonderen Verwendung 1

Stab KGzbV.1 (Loddenheide) – Oberstleutnant Fritz
Morzik) (1× Ju 52/3m/3m)

I./KGzbV.1 (Werl) – Major Karl Georg Witt
(51× Ju 52/3m/3m)

II./KGzbV.1 (Loddenheide) – Major Karl Drewes
(53× Ju 52/3m/3m)

III./KGzbV.1 (Handorf) – Hauptmann Markus Zeidler
(50× Ju 52/3m/3m)

IV./KGzbV.1 (Loddenheide) – Major Beckmann
(53× Ju 52/3m/3m)

Kampfgeschwader zur besonderen Verwendung 2

Stab KGzbV.2 (Lippspringe) – Oberstleutnant Gerhard
Conrad (1× Ju 52/3m/3m)

KGrzbV.9 (Lippspringe) – Major Johann Janzen
(53× Ju 52/3m/3m)

KGrzbV.11 (Lippstadt) – Hauptmann Hans-Eberhard
Freiherr von Hornbach (51× Ju 52/3m/3m)

KGrzbV.12 (Störmede) – Oberstleutnant Gustav Wilke
(51× Ju 52/3m/3m)

I./KGrzbV.172 (Paderborn) – Hauptmann Krause
(48× Ju 52/3m/3m)

Fernaufklärungsstaffel II. Flakkorps (Köln) – Oberleutnant
Langhuth (3× Do 17M; 4× Hs 126B)

Aufklärungsstaffel zbV (Gütersloh) – Oberleutnant Florin
(5× Do 17M)

Sonderstaffel Schwilden/KGr.zbV.108 (Bad
Zwischenahn) – Hauptmann Horst Schwilden
(12× He 59D)

9.Fliegerdivsion (Jever) – Generalmajor J. Coeler

Kampfgruppe 126 (Marx) – Hauptmann Gerd Stein
(24× He 111H)

3./Küstenfliegergruppe 106 (Borkum) – Hauptmann
Kannengiesser (10× He 115 B/C)

3./Küstenfliegergruppe 506 (Norderney) – Hauptmann
Bergemann (11× He 115 B/C)

3./Küstenfliegergruppe 906 (Norderney) – Hauptmann
Klumper (7× He 115B)

DEFENDER'S CAPABILITIES
The Dutch defences

From roughly the 1840s to 1940, Dutch governments maintained a diplomatic policy of strict neutrality in the hope that the nation would not become drawn into a large-scale conflict between the Great Powers, provided it did not antagonize either side. Alongside this diplomatic policy ran an overall military strategy of 'armed neutrality' which reasoned that sufficiently powerful armed forces had to be maintained to protect national sovereignty, in the event of an attack by a Great Power, long enough for an opposing Great Power to come to Dutch assistance. Great strategic stock was held in the belief that one Great Power would not want to drive the Netherlands into the arms of another Great Power in a general European conflict. On the ground, this policy translated into a series of extensive fortifications: the aforementioned Vesting Holland, and later-constructed Grebbelinie, Peel-Raamstelling, and Waterlinie.

To supplement the fortifications and their garrisons, a standing *Veldleger*, or field army, was established in the late nineteenth century. It was intended that this force could be mobilized quickly and then rapidly deployed to conflict areas outside of the Vesting Holland, stabilizing breaches in any of the outer defence lines.

When the Dutch *Luchtvaartafdeeling der Koninklijke Landmacht* (LVA), or Air Service of the Royal Dutch Army, was established in 1913, its role was likewise strictly defensive. During World War I, while the Veldleger patrolled the nation's borders, the LVA was tasked with defending Dutch skies from incursions by belligerent aircraft so that combatants could not accuse the Netherlands of allowing Dutch air space to be used by one side or the other. This mission was performed with great difficulty as the Netherlands did not yet have a capable domestic aircraft industry and was reliant upon aircraft purchased abroad or interned belligerent aircraft impressed into Dutch service.

Highly manoeuvrable for a twin-engine fighter and possessing a powerful armament of eight machine guns, the Fokker G.1A was an unpleasant surprise for Luftwaffe pilots. Luftwaffe planners had not effectively evaluated the capabilities of this aircraft prior to Unternehmen F. This G.1A replica, photographed in its previous home at the Militaire Luchtvaart Museum in Soesterberg, is now stored at the Nationaal Militair Museum in Soest. (Author's collection)

Dutch military aircraft in the 1930s

By the early 1930s, the LVA was largely a token force, composed of a single *Jachtvliegtuigafdeeling* (JaVA), or fighter squadron, made up of Fokker D.XVI and D.XVII biplane fighters, two

Petrus Wilhelmus Best (front row, middle), as a Generaal-Majoor and commander of the Wapen der Militaire Luchtvaart (MI), or Dutch military air service, photographed with the staff of the Commando Luchtverdediging, or Dutch air defence command, in front of its headquarters in Den Haag. (Collectie Nederlands Instituut voor Militaire Historie)

OPPOSITE
Fokker company preliminary diagram of its T.V luchtkruiser, or air cruiser, a Dutch variation on the late 1920s Multiplace de Combat multi-role aircraft concept. While the heavy battleplane concept had largely been discarded by 1940, the ML's T.Vs surprisingly served in their originally intended role during the early hours of the Meidagen campaign (literally 'May Days'; Dutch term for the five-day German campaign to occupy the Netherlands). (Courtesy of the Aviation Museum Aviodrome, Netherlands)

army-cooperation groups consisting of Fokker C.V multi-purpose biplanes, and a training squadron possessing three Fokker F.VIIa/3m transport/bombers and other trainers. The LVA had only one permanent ground installation and airfield at Soesterberg, just east of Utrecht, at which these units were based.

The rise of Hitler in Germany and the failure of the League of Nations to effectively counter Japanese, Italian, and later German military aggression created new defence concerns which the small LVA was unsuited to face. *Luitenant-kolonel* Petrus Wilhelmus Best, who was appointed commander of the LVA on November 1, 1933, immediately recognized his service's shortcomings against the rising tide of militarism and rearmament sweeping across the Continent in the mid-1930s. In large part due to Best's lobbying, the *Inspectie der Militaire Luchtvaart* (Military Aviation Inspectorate) or IML was formed in April 1935 under the leadership of Generaal-majoor Marius Raaijmakers. The IML sought to remedy the poor operational status of the LVA, create a modern aircraft procurement programme, and construct new airfields in order to effectively disperse and service its aircraft. Despite lingering economic fallout from the Great Depression, the government of Minister-President Hendrik Colijn recognized the pressing need for increased military funding and on February 18, 1936, passed a new Defence Fund which prioritized funding for new aircraft and anti-aircraft gun acquisition.

With funding in place, in early 1937 the IML published its plan to expand the LVA to a size necessary to meet the new objectives of an updated armed neutrality strategy, given the advances in technology and change of strategies and tactics after World War I. The IML's plan detailed the types of aircraft required, the specifications of which were immediately issued to Dutch aircraft manufacturers, and laid out a new aircraft acquisition plan, intended to get the LVA to its recommended size within four years.

The new LVA structure created by the IML consisted of the *1e Luchtvaartregiment* (1 LvR), or 1st Aviation Regiment, which was tasked with air defence. It would be made up of two reconnaissance squadrons, three bomber squadrons, and four fighter squadrons (two with single-engine interceptors and two with twin-engine *jachtkruisers,* or heavy fighters). The 2e Luchtvaartregiment (2 LvR) was tasked with supporting the Veldleger and was made up of four reconnaissance groups and *Jachtgroep Veldleger*, or Field Army Fighter Group (four fighter squadrons, two with single engine interceptors and two with twin-engine jachtkruisers). A third Luchtvaartregiment (3 LvR) was tasked with training for 1 LvR and 2 LvR and was composed of three training squadrons; one elementary, one intermediate, and one advanced. It is interesting to note that at the time the LVA regarded the reconnaissance of and the bombing of advancing enemy ground forces as part of the air defence role, hence the reconnaissance and bomber squadrons assigned to 1 LvR. Each fighter, bomber, and reconnaissance squadron in 1 LvR and 2 LvR's Jachgroep Veldleger was allotted 18 aircraft: nine operational and nine to be kept in reserve. The four reconnaissance groups in 2 LvR would each receive 18 reconnaissance aircraft and 12 light multi-purpose aircraft.

The first aircraft acquired according to the IML's four-year plan were for the 1ᵉ Luchtvaartregiment and initially the Ministry of Defence insisted that new aircraft be purchased by domestic manufacturers. At the time, only the Fokker company, formally known as the *Nederlandsche Vliegtuigenfabriek*, was equipped to deliver sizeable orders of aircraft.

Anthony Fokker had re-established his formerly German company in the Netherlands following the internal collapse and revolution in Germany in 1919, and continued to be a major designer and manufacturer of competitive military and commercial aircraft throughout the interwar years. As it had been the primary manufacturer of aircraft for the LVA throughout the 1920s and early 1930s, the LVA turned to Fokker for its new generation of aircraft.

The first of the four-year plan aircraft ordered was the Fokker T.V *luchtkruiser*, or air cruiser; the luchtkruiser concept was a Dutch variation on the late 1920s *Multiplace de Combat* multi-role aircraft designation which was studied by several air forces during the interwar years. In the LVA's understanding, the luchtkruiser could serve both as a medium bomber in offensive missions and in a defensive role

as a heavily-armed battleplane that could wade into and attack enemy bomber formations.

On 4 January 1937, the Ministry of Defence placed an initial order for 16 T.Vs from Fokker to form an initial bomber squadron with nine operational aircraft, six in reserve, and one to be used by the advanced training squadron. Construction began on the first aircraft in February 1937, and it made its first flight on October 16. The production T.V was powered by two 925hp Bristol Pegasus XXVI radials, had a payload of 2,205lb, and was armed with four 7.9mm FN Browning defensive machine guns. The aircraft's primary weapon was its 20mm Solothurn cannon, mounted in the nose; such was the LVA's insistence upon the luchtkruiser concept that the forward gunner/bombardier, rather than the pilot, was made the commander of each T.V crew. The lengthy development and production time for the T.V meant that it was surpassed by foreign medium bomber projects when it finally entered service in numbers in early 1939 and already in early 1938 the LVA was looking for a more competitive bomber.

Anthony Fokker and his aircraft company had great success with domestic and export sales throughout the 1920s but he was slow to adapt to all-metal construction methods. As a result, his sales waned throughout the early and mid-1930s. European rearmament in the late 1930s again increased sales and a new design team, coupled with updated construction techniques, led to a rapid modernization of designs. Fokker died of meningitis unexpectedly in December 1939 but by that time his company had state-of-the-art aircraft designs entering the prototype phase. Fokker (front row, third from left) is seen here in 1931 in Berlin with pilot friends from World War I, Bruno Loerzer (far left) and Ernst Udet (front row, fourth from left), both of whom would later become generals in the Luftwaffe. (Courtesy of the Aviation Museum Aviodrome, Netherlands)

Fokker T.V	
Length:	53ft 1¾in (16.2m)
Wingspan:	68ft 10¾in (21m)
Powerplant:	2 x 925hp Bristol Pegasus XXVI radials
Maximum speed:	264mph (425km/h)
Ceiling:	26,247ft (8,000m)
Range:	963 miles (1,550km)
Armament:	1 x 20mm Solothurn cannon, 4 x 7.9mm Mitrailleur M.20 Vliegtuig machine guns, 2,205lb (1,000kg) of bombs
Crew:	5

For a single-engine interceptor fighter for the 1 LvR's first two fighter squadrons, the Ministry of Defence ordered 36 Fokker D.XXI monoplane fighters on 31 December 1937. The D.XXI was initially designed to a 1934 request from the *Luchtvaartafdeling van het Koninklijk Nederlands-Indisch Leger* (Royal Netherlands East Indies Army Air Service) and did not impress Kolonel Best when the prototype was demonstrated before him in February 1936. Its 645hp Bristol Mercury VI-S engine gave the aircraft a maximum speed which was only 25mph faster than the biplane fighters in LVA service at the time.

Best was not inclined to purchase the aircraft when the four-year plan began but the Ministry of Defence requested that the LVA re-evaluate the design as Fokker was in the process of producing an improved version of the aircraft for Finland. This aircraft, powered by an 840hp Bristol Mercury VIII radial and armed with four 7.9mm FN Browning machine guns in its wings, had a more respectable maximum speed and, with its mixed welded steel tube/wood/fabric construction, was highly manoeuvrable. The mixed construction also resulted in a price tag significantly lower than those of all-metal construction, making it a seemingly prudent immediate purchase. Anachronistically, the D.XXI had fixed landing gear but the pilots that tested it thought it was a technological leap from their previous biplanes. The LVA's D.XXIs were delivered between August 1938 and April 1939. The rapid pace of technological development abroad meant that the D.XXI would not remain a competitive interceptor for long, so the LVA had already decided in 1938 to transfer its D.XXIs to the

Although much slower than and not as heavily armed as the Bf 109, the superior manoeuvrability of the Fokker D.XXI would make it a competitive opponent in turning dogfights during the Meidagen. This D.XXI replica, photographed in the previous Militaire Luchtvaart Museum in Soesterberg, is now on display at the Nationaal Militair Museum in Soest. (Author's collection)

two fighter squadrons of the Jachtgroep Veldleger once a superior interceptor was available for purchase.

Fokker D.XXI	
Length:	26ft 11in (8.2m)
Wingspan:	36ft 1in (11m)
Powerplant:	1 x 840hp Bristol Mercury VIII radial
Maximum speed:	286mph (460km/h)
Ceiling:	33,137ft (10,100m)
Range:	578 miles (930km)
Armament:	4 x 7.9mm FN Browning M36 machine guns

The aircraft under development at Fokker which Best was most eager to acquire was the Fokker G.1 *jachtkruiser*, a revolutionary design which was a domestic and international sensation when unveiled to the world at the Salon de l'Aéronautique in Paris in November 1936. The jachtkruiser, or fighter cruiser, concept was a twin-engine heavy fighter that could also perform the roles of fighter-bomber and long-range reconnaissance aircraft.

The production version of the G.1 had a large wing with a small fuselage in the centre, twin tail booms, and was powered by two 800hp Bristol Mercury VIII radials, similar to the engine used in the D.XXI; this was a purposeful choice as the LVA hoped to simplify powerplant logistics in its fighters through the use of a single engine. The heavy fighter's armament was perhaps its most impressive feature: initially armed with two 23mm Madsen cannon and two 7.9mm Madsen machine guns, the LVA decided to arm the aircraft with eight 7.9mm FN Browning machine guns in the nose and a single one in the rear nose. The G.1 was also of mixed construction like the T.V and D.XXI, and demonstrated surprising manoeuvrability for a larger aircraft when the prototype was tested throughout the spring and summer of 1937.

Best was so impressed with the G.1 that he wanted to equip all of his fighter squadrons with it, believing that it was superior in the interceptor role than the D.XXI; his more-conservative superiors in the Ministry of Defence were unsure of relying exclusively on such a revolutionary design and compelled Best to divide his initial fighter orders between the D.XXI and G.1. That being said, the Ministry of Defence placed an order for 36 Fokker G.1As on December 31, 1937, and these were delivered from November 1938 through October 1939.

Fokker G.1A	
Length:	35ft 9in (10.9m)
Wingspan:	56ft 5in (17.2m)
Powerplant:	2 x 800hp Bristol Mercury VIII radials
Maximum speed:	295mph (475km/h)
Ceiling:	30,840ft (9,400m)
Range:	932 miles (1,500km)
Armament:	8 x 7.9mm FN Browning M36 machine guns
Crew:	2

By the end of 1937, enough new aircraft had been ordered to equip a bomber squadron and four fighter squadrons, and in May 1938 the Minister of Defence requested a list of recommended purchases from the IML for the remainder of squadrons yet to be equipped under the four-year plan. The IML requested the opportunity to recommend aircraft from foreign manufacturers, due to design and production delays at Fokker, and this was granted.

OPPOSITE MILITAIRE LUCHTVAART PRIMARY AND AUXILIARY AIRFIELDS IN USE ON 10 MAY 1940, AND COMMANDO LUCHTVERDEDIGING PRIMARY AIR DEFENCE SECTORS

After the beginning of World War II, the ML had dispersed its squadrons to a number of newly built military airfields, civilian airports, commandeered flying clubs, or auxiliary airfields. The map shows the airfields where ML aircraft were stationed on 10 May 1940 (*see pp. 26 for the ML's order of battle*). In addition to the squadrons of the 1ᵉ Luchtvaartregiment assigned to air defence, the Commando Luchtverdediging also controlled the ground-to-air defences stationed throughout the country. The Brigade Luchtdoelartillerie possessed 273 modern and 39 obsolete anti-aircraft guns, and 452 machine guns designated for anti-aircraft use. The Brigade Luchtdoelartillerie's batteries were divided up among eight air defence sectors and a number were assigned to the Veldleger (IIᵉ, IIIᵉ, and IVᵉ Legerkorps) and the Iᵉ Legerkorps. Throughout the Meidagen, Dutch anti-aircraft fire proved to be much more lethal to Luftwaffe aircraft than the fighters of the ML; anti-aircraft fire accounted for roughly 50–60 per cent of all Luftwaffe losses over the Netherlands. The distribution of the Brigade Luchtdoelartillerie's guns is shown on the map.

Dissatisfied with the D.XXI as an interceptor, Best and the IML examined the Hawker Hurricane, Supermarine Spitfire, and a variant of the Heinkel He 112B powered by a Daimler-Benz engine. In the Netherlands, Fokker and the smaller De Schelde aviation firm were also developing designs for state-of-the-art interceptors, the Fokker D.XXIII and De Schelde S.21, which both had twin booms and a pusher configuration (the D.XXIII additionally had a second engine in a tractor configuration). Also under consideration was the FK 58 monoplane, a refined version of the Fokker D.XXI design, being developed by the Dutch *Vliegtuigenfabriek Koolhoven*. The IML recommended the purchase of 36 Dornier Do 215 (export version of the Do 17Z) high-speed bombers to serve as both bombers and strategic reconnaissance aircraft for 1 LvR's reconnaissance squadrons. For the two jachtkruiser squadrons intended for the Jachtgroep Veldleger, multi-purpose heavy fighter designs from Fokker, Koolhoven, and De Schelde were considered, along with the Douglas DB-8A/3N light bomber/ground attack aircraft already in production in the United States.

Development and production delays, budgetary arguments between the LVA and the Minister of Defence, and the inability to acquire aircraft from belligerent nations after the start of World War II in September 1939 resulted in almost none of these aircraft being acquired for Dutch squadrons by May 1940; only 18 Douglas DB-8A/3Ns and 26 partially finished Fokker G.1B jachtkruisers (a smaller export version of the G.1, powered by Pratt & Whitney Twin Wasp Jr. engines and armed with only four machine guns) were purchased prior to the German invasion.

Although the LVA did not receive the full complement of modern aircraft envisioned by the IML's four-year plan, Kolonel Best and the IML had significantly improved the combat potential of Dutch squadrons since Best took command in 1933. On 1 November 1938, in a further improvement for the LVA, Minister of Defence van Dijk created the *Commando Luchtverdediging* (C.-Lvd.), or Air Defence Command, and the newly-promoted *Generaal-Majoor* Best was named as its commander.

The Commando Luchtverdediging, with a central headquarters in Den Haag, encompassed all units associated with air defence including the fighter, bomber, and reconnaissance squadrons of the 1ᵉ Luchtvaartregiment, the *Luchtvaartbrigade* (depot, technical and airfield garrison units), the *Brigade Luchtdoelartillerie* (anti-aircraft batteries), the *3e Regiment Genietroepen* (searchlight engineer units), the *Luchtwachtdienst* (air observation service), and the *Vrijwillig Landstormkorps Luchtwachtdienst*, or volunteer reserve air observation service. The 2ᵉ Luchtvaartregiment, which consisted mostly of reconnaissance units, remained under the command of the Veldleger. This was a long-overdue development as before this the Netherlands had few effective anti-aircraft guns and no coordinated air defence network.

Upon the C.-Lvd.'s creation, Best immediately went to work placing orders for hundreds of modern anti-aircraft guns from both domestic and foreign manufacturers. By May 1940, the

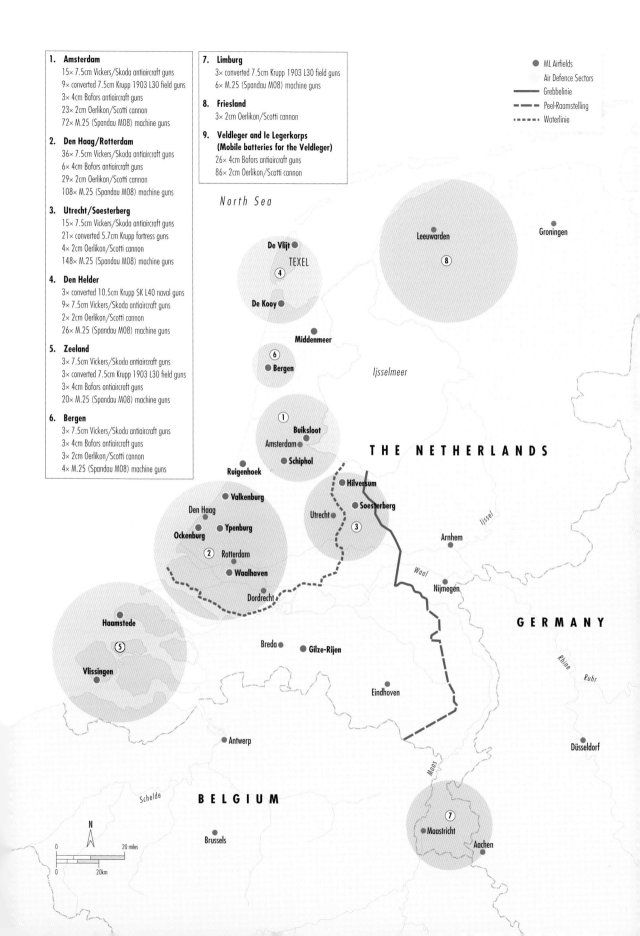

1. **Amsterdam**
    15× 7.5cm Vickers/Skoda antiaircraft guns
    9× converted 7.5cm Krupp 1903 L30 field guns
    3× 4cm Bofors antiaircraft guns
    23× 2cm Oerlikon/Scotti cannon
    72× M.25 (Spandau M08) machine guns

2. **Den Haag/Rotterdam**
    36× 7.5cm Vickers/Skoda antiaircraft guns
    6× 4cm Bofors antiaircraft guns
    29× 2cm Oerlikon/Scotti cannon
    108× M.25 (Spandau M08) machine guns

3. **Utrecht/Soesterberg**
    15× 7.5cm Vickers/Skoda antiaircraft guns
    21× converted 5.7cm Krupp fortress guns
    4× 2cm Oerlikon/Scotti cannon
    148× M.25 (Spandau M08) machine guns

4. **Den Helder**
    3× converted 10.5cm Krupp SK L40 naval guns
    9× 7.5cm Vickers/Skoda antiaircraft guns
    2× 2cm Oerlikon/Scotti cannon
    26× M.25 (Spandau M08) machine guns

5. **Zeeland**
    3× 7.5cm Vickers/Skoda antiaircraft guns
    3× converted 7.5cm Krupp 1903 L30 field guns
    3× 4cm Bofors antiaircraft guns
    20× M.25 (Spandau M08) machine guns

6. **Bergen**
    3× 7.5cm Vickers/Skoda antiaircraft guns
    3× 4cm Bofors antiaircraft guns
    3× 2cm Oerlikon/Scotti cannon
    4× M.25 (Spandau M08) machine guns

7. **Limburg**
    3× converted 7.5cm Krupp 1903 L30 field guns
    6× M.25 (Spandau M08) machine guns

8. **Friesland**
    3× 2cm Oerlikon/Scotti cannon

9. **Veldleger and Ie Legerkorps**
    (Mobile batteries for the Veldleger)
    26× 4cm Bofors antiaircraft guns
    86× 2cm Oerlikon/Scotti cannon

● ML Airfields
○ Air Defence Sectors
── Grebbelinie
─ ─ Peel-Raamstelling
····· Waterlinie

North Sea

De Vlijt ●
TEXEL
④

De Kooy ●

Middenmeer ●

Leeuwarden ●
⑧

Groningen ●

Ijsselmeer

⑥
Bergen ●

①
Buiksloot ●
Amsterdam
Schiphol ●

THE NETHERLANDS

Ruigenhoek ●

Valkenburg ●
Den Haag ●
Ypenburg ●
Ockenburg ●
②
Rotterdam
Waalhaven ●

Dordrecht ●

Hilversum ●
Soesterberg ●
Utrecht ●
③

Arnhem ●

Ijssel

Waal

Nijmegen ●

GERMANY

Haamstede ●
⑤
Vlissingen ●

Breda ●
Gilze-Rijen ●

Eindhoven ●

Rhine
Ruhr

Antwerp ●

Schelde

BELGIUM

Brussels ●

Maas

⑦
Maastricht ●
Aachen ●

Düsseldorf ●

N

0   20 miles
0   20km

C.-Lvd. received 155 Oerlikon and Scotti Isotta Fraschini 2cm guns, 46 Bofors 4cm guns, and 72 Vickers 7.5cm guns, and their accompanying fire control systems.

Best also oversaw the set-up of an effective telephone communication network, connecting the Vrijwillig Landstormkorps Luchtwachtdienst's 146 observation posts to the *Centraal Luchtwachtbureau*, or Central Air Observation Office. This office disseminated incoming reports and passed them on to the C.-Lvd.'s headquarters, which then, through direct telephone lines or radio receivers, alerted appropriate squadrons or anti-aircraft batteries. Experiments were under way in early 1940 in which the C.-Lvd. vectored Dutch aircraft toward incoming 'bogies' by radio but this was not standard practice by May 1940 as not all Dutch aircraft were equipped with radios by then. Shortly before the war the C.-Lvd. also experimented with an early radar set, being developed by the Philips electronics firm in Eindhoven, which could detect aircraft up to 18km away.

Marius Beeling (left), the chief engineer at Fokker when World War II began, standing in front of the Fokker D.XXIII advanced twin-engine pusher/puller fighter prototype. By the end of 1939, both the Fokker and De Schelde aviation firms were developing prototypes for new fighters which would have rivalled the best of other foreign manufacturers. The German invasion brought an abrupt end to these promising developments. To the right of Beeling is Fokker test pilot Gerben Sonderman, who as a G.1A pilot in the 3ᵉ JaVA scored more kills than any other ML pilot during the Meidagen. (Courtesy of the Aviation Museum Aviodrome, Netherlands)

Best's plans for a modern, integrated air defence network were not complete by May 1940 but he had created the most sophisticated and effective air defence system in western Europe, much more advanced than anything the larger armed forces of France and Belgium could boast. On 1 July 1939, all of the former LVA squadrons and the Commando Luchtverdediging's organizations were formed into the *Wapen der Militaire Luchtvaart*, or simply the Militaire Luchtvaart (ML), with Best as its commander.

Dutch Brigade Luchtdoelartillerie (anti-aircraft brigade) troops training on a 7.5cm Vickers/Skoda anti-aircraft gun, stationed at Bergen Airfield. (Courtesy of the Douglas Dildy Collection)

War looms

In spite of a declaration of neutrality at the beginning of the war and Hitler's promise that Germany would respect Dutch neutrality, the government and armed forces of the Netherlands were sceptical of German promises by January 1940. Despite German attempts at secrecy, various intelligence sources suggested German offensive action against Dutch territory as well as the possible use of airborne units. The *Generale Staf sectie III* (GS III), the intelligence service of the Koninklijke Leger, maintained mobile listening posts which disseminated Wehrmacht radio traffic on a routine basis. It had broken parts of the Wehrmacht's codes and notably the code of the German *Auswärtiges Amt*, or foreign office. Dutch businessmen and KLM pilots travelling through Germany, who were GS III agents, brought back reports of suspicious troop concentrations and exercises throughout the winter and spring of 1940. The increasing frequency of German reconnaissance flights in the months leading up to May and suspected Lufthansa photographic flights were an ominous portent as well.

GS III also had a special 'ace-in-the-hole'; the Dutch military attaché in Berlin, Major Gijsbertus Sas, received clandestine intelligence data from Oberst Hans Oster, deputy chief of the German *Abwehr*, the Wehrmacht's intelligence service, and leading figure among the German resistance to Hitler and the Nazis. Oster routinely updated Sas as to the pending execution dates for Fall Gelb, but due to the plans' numerous cancellations and rescheduling throughout, Sas' warnings eventually began to fall on deaf ears within the Koninklijke Leger's leadership. Prime Minister Dirk Jan de Geer, who was insistent upon giving the Germans no excuse to violate Dutch neutrality, refused to take any pre-emptive steps against a possible German invasion.

Oster did inform Sas in advance of Unternehmen Weserübung, the German invasion of Denmark and Norway on 9 April 1940, and when this took place on the day Oster specified, the Dutch military leadership began to reconsider the reports coming from Sas. Generaal Best in particular was concerned about the use of heavily armed German infantry, flown in by transport aircraft, in the capture and securing of Fornebu Airport in Oslo on 9 April. The operation was witnessed first-hand by KLM pilot Evert van Dijk, also a GS III agent who happened to be on a routine flight there; van Dijk extensively briefed Best on what he saw on his return to the Netherlands. The details of this operation fell into place with other pieces of intelligence suggesting German offensive action against Dutch airfields and Best immediately increased the security details at his airfields. All combat squadrons were withdrawn to airfields within the Vesting Holland and obstacles were placed around the unused areas of airfields as well as sections of highways which transport aircraft might use

In the centre background of the photograph is KLM's DC-3 airliner *Kemphaan*, which happened to be on a routine flight at Fornebu Airport at Oslo on 9 April 1940 when the Germans captured the airport in a daring airlanding operation. *Kemphaan*'s pilot, Evert van Dijk, was a member of the Dutch GS III intelligence service and, upon his return to Schiphol, provided a valuable eyewitness account of the tactics used by German troopers, rapidly deploying from Ju 52/3m transports. Van Dijk's report played an important role in improving airfield defences in the Netherlands prior to the coming German invasion. (Collectie Nederlands Instituut voor Militaire Historie)

for landing. On April 22, Best briefed his airfield commanders about the full details of the German operation at Oslo and ordered them to prepare contingency plans for the effective defence of their airfields. Best also ordered his combat squadrons to have patrols ready to scramble, if needed, at dawn on every morning.

Despite the accuracy of Oster's intelligence regarding the invasion of Denmark and Norway and the ominous events at Oslo, elements of the Dutch civilian and military leadership still vainly hoped to maintain Dutch neutrality and refused more proactive defensive preparations beyond what Best had already done on his own initiative. Given that, the Commando Luchtverdediging and its squadrons were as ready as they could be on the evening of 9 May when Sas phoned from Berlin, instructing GS III that Oster warned him that Fall Gelb would be executed at dawn the following morning and that this time the counter-order had not been issued.

ORDER OF BATTLE, 10 MAY 1040

Units of the Militaire Luchtvaart
Wapen het Militaire Luchtvaart (Den Haag) –
Generaal-majoor Petrus Wilhelmus Best
1e Luchtvaartregiment (Schiphol) – Majoor H.G. van Voorthuijsen
Strategische Groep (Schiphol) – Majoor J.T.H. van Weeren
Strategische Verkenningsvliegtuig Afdeling, or StratVerVA (Bergen) – Kapitein J. van der Werff (10x Fokker C.X)
Bombardeervliegtuigafdeeling, or BomVA (Schiphol) – Kapitein J.G.Sissingh (9x Fokker T.V)
Jachtgroep (Den Haag) – Majoor H. van Weerden Poelman
1e Jachtvliegtuigafdeeling, or 1e JaVA (De Kooy) – Kapitein H.M. Schmidt Crans (11x Fokker D.XXI)
2e Jachtvliegtuigafdeeling, or 2e JaVA (Schiphol) – Kapitein P.J.E. Janssens (9x Fokker D.XXI)
3e Jachtvliegtuigafdeeling, or 3e JaVA (Waalhaven) – Kapitein H. J. Scholtmeijer (11x Fokker G.1A)
4e Jachtvliegtuigafdeeling, or 4e JaVA (Bergen) – Kapitein T.J.A. Lamers (12x Fokker G.1A)

2e Luchtvaartregiment (Zeist) – Luitenant-kolonel J.H. Sar
Ie Verkenningsgroep, or Ie Verk.Gr. (Hilversum) – Majoor H. van der Zanden (1x Fokker C.X; 4x Fokker C.V; 4x Koolhoven FK 51)
IIe Verkenningsgroep, or IIe Verk.Gr. (Ypenburg) – Kapitein H.L.G. Lambert (7x Fokker C.V; 5x Koolhoven FK 51)
IIIe Verkenningsgroep, or IIIe Verk.Gr. (Ruigenhoek) – Majoor F. Raland (9x Fokker C.V; 4x Koolhoven FK 51)

IVe Verkenningsgroep, or IVe Verk.Gr. (Gilze-Rijen) - Kapitein A.W. de Ruyter van Steveninck (7x Fokker C.V; 3x Koolhoven FK 51)
Jachtgroep Veldleger, or Ve Jachtgroep (Ockenburg) – Kapitein W.H. Wijnkamp
1e Afdeling van de Jachtgroep Veldleger, or 1-V-2 (Ypenburg) – 1e Luitenant P.J.B. Ruijs de Perez (8x Fokker D.XXI)
3e Afdeling van de Jachtgroep Veldleger, or 3-V-2 (Ypenburg) – Kapitein J.A. Bach (11x Douglas DB-8A/3N)

3e Luchtvaartregiment (De Vlijt) – Kapitein J. L. Zegers
Elementaire Vliegschool (Vlissingen) (11x Fokker S.IV; 17x Fokker S.IX)
Voortgezette Vliegschool (Haamstede) (9x Fokker C.V; 1x Fokker C.IX; 1x Fokker F.VIIA; 10x Koolhoven FK 51; 2x Koolhoven FK 56)
Jachtvliegschool (De Vlijt) (1x Bücker BU 131; 1x Fokker D.XVI; 7x Fokker D.XVII; 2x Fokker D.XXI; 1x Fokker G.1A; 1x Fokker S.II; 1x Fokker T.V; 2x Focke-Wulf Fw58B-2; 3x Koolhoven FK 56; 1x North American NA27)

Author's Note
Both the German and Dutch orders of battle only include aircraft that were at operational status on 10 May 1940. Also note, not included in the Dutch order of battle are the 101 aircraft, mostly floatplanes and trainers of the Marine Luchtvaartdienst (Naval Air Service), or MLD, of the Koninklijke Marine (Royal Netherlands Navy); these aircraft did not participate in combat during the Meidagen, or May Days (the colloquial Dutch name for the Netherlands Campaign in 1940), in any significant way.

CAMPAIGN OBJECTIVES
Unternehmen F

With the method of attack determined as well as targets selected from the extensive reconnaissance missions, Göring, Kesselring, Student, and von Sponeck presented their final plan for Unternehmen F to Hitler on 2 May 1940, who in turn approved it the following day. On May 8, Kesselring, Student, and Sponeck presented the full plan to their subordinates. The prerequisite of air superiority over the Vesting Holland for any chance of success for the subsequent airborne and airlanding operations was not lost on Kesselring and neither was the importance of the element of surprise.

Kesselring had been involved in the Luftwaffe's campaign of air superiority over Poland, which was achieved by the end of the first week of the invasion through sustained attacks on Polish airfields the Polish air force's logistics infrastructure. The combat aircraft of the Polish air force were not destroyed on the ground however as they had been successfully dispersed and camouflaged when the Poles mobilized on 29 September 1939, two days before the German attack. While Polish aerial resistance was largely ineffective and could not be conducted en masse, it was a nuisance and inflicted losses upon the Luftwaffe.

Attempting to learn from the Polish experience, emphasis was especially placed upon the element of surprise for the aerial attack on Dutch airfields. In a *ruse de guerre*, the initial Luftwaffe bomber sorties would fly from their bases out into the North Sea and head to the northwest of the Netherlands, giving the impression to Dutch observers that they were on their way to Great Britain for a raid. Once outside visual range of the Dutch coast, roughly 15–20 miles to the west, the bombers would turn south, parallel to the Dutch coast, and then turn east towards their targets. The bombers would then fly to their targets at low altitude so that their approach would not be spotted until the last minute by airfield defences; it was anticipated that a low-altitude approach from the west would catch the defenders by surprise. The timings of the initial attacks on the airfields also had to be coordinated as closely as possible to minimize any warning given to other targets and hence the defenders' response time to prepare countermeasures.

The Willemsbrug road bridge across the Nieuwe Maas in Rotterdam, seen here just to the left of the railway bridge on the left side of the photo, was a key objective of Student's Fallschirmjäger landing around Waalhaven. The bridge was needed intact if the panzers of the 9.Panzer-Division were to advance on Den Haag and Amsterdam. Some of the most intense fighting of the campaign took place in the streets and buildings adjacent to the Willemsbrug. (Collectie Nederlands Instituut voor Militaire Historie)

OPPOSITE LUFTFLOTTE 2 HOME AIRFIELDS AND TARGETS IN THE NETHERLANDS AT THE BEGINNING OF UNTERNEHMEN F, WITH ATTACKS BEGINNING AT 0355HRS, 10 MAY 1940

In the final Luftwaffe plan for Unternehmen F, the bid to achieve air superiority over the Vesting Holland was left to General Putzier's Fliegerkorps zbV.2. Putzier decided that, if surprise could be achieved, an initial heavy blow against the ML's airfields with the majority of his bombers gave the best hopes of destroying its strength, hopefully on the ground. Putzier formed an initial bombing wave that would circle around the Netherlands, via the North Sea as suggested by Kesselring, and attack its targets from the west. The aircraft assigned to this first bombing wave were to remain off the Dutch coast until 0350hrs and then all head for their targets simultaneously. A number of secondary targets, primarily airfields where aircraft not considered front-line were based, were assigned as part of the mission of a first wave of fighters, flying directly from their bases in Germany. Other fighters in this first wave would take station over a predesignated patrol area and perform bomber escort, combat air patrol, and what would later be termed *Freie Jagd* – or free hunt – fighter sweeps as needed.

The latter type of fighter mission was not yet specifically defined at this time in the war as the Luftwaffe was still in the process of honing operational strategies for its single- and twin-engine fighters. In addition to previously assigned fighter units, General Döring was loaned the II.(J)/Tr.Gr.186, IV.(N)/JG 2, and 2./ZG 76 from Jagdfliegerführer Deutsche Bucht for these early-morning missions. Putzier had saved his Gruppe of Stukas for a thorough neutralization of the anti-aircraft and ground defences around the road and rail bridges at Moerdijk as their capture was absolutely essential to the success of Unternehmen F.

Generalmajor Kurt-Bertram von Döring, commander of Jagdfliegerführer 2, which made up almost all of Luftflotte 2's fighter units. (Author's collection)

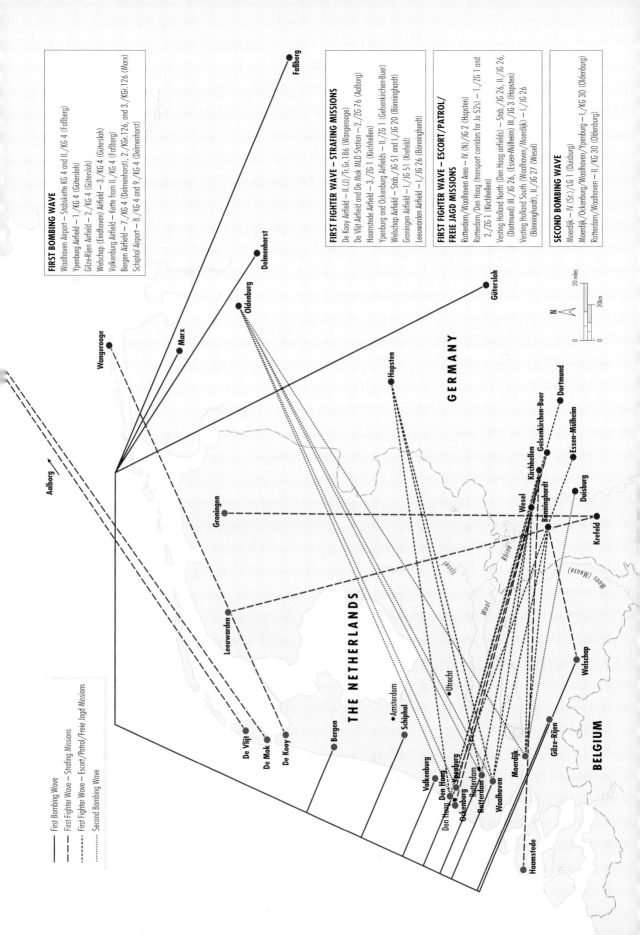

FIRST BOMBING WAVE

Waalhaven Airport – Stabskette KG 4 and II./KG 4 (Faßberg)
Ypenburg Airfield – 1./KG 4 (Gütersloh)
Gilze-Rijen Airfield – 2./KG 4 (Gütersloh)
Welschap (Eindhoven) Airfield – 3./KG 4 (Gütersloh)
Valkenburg Airfield – Kette from II./KG 4 (Faßberg)
Bergen Airfield – 7./KG 4 (Delmenhorst), 2./KGr.126, and 3./KGr.126 (Marx)
Schiphol Airport – 8./KG 4 and 9./KG 4 (Delmenhorst)

FIRST FIGHTER WAVE – STRAFING MISSIONS

De Kooy Airfield – II.(J)/Tr.Gr.186 (Wangerooge)
De Vlijt Airfield and De Mok MLD Station – 2./ZG 76 (Aalborg)
Haamstede Airfield – 3./ZG 1 (Kirchhellen)
Ypenburg and Ockenburg Airfields – II./ZG 1 (Gelsenkirchen-Buer)
Welschop Airfield – Stab./JG 51 and I./JG 20 (Bönninghardt)
Groningen Airfield – I./JG 51 (Krefeld)
Leeuwarden Airfield – I./JG 26 (Bönninghardt)

**FIRST FIGHTER WAVE – ESCORT/PATROL/
FREIE JAGD MISSIONS**

Rotterdam/Waalhoven Area – IV.(N)/JG 2 (Hopsten)
Rotterdam/Den Haag (transport corridors for Ju 52s) – I./ZG 1 and
2./ZG 1 (Kirchhellen)
Vesting Holland North (Den Haag airfields) – Stab./JG 26, II./JG 26,
(Dortmund) III./JG 26, (Essen-Mülheim) III./JG 3 (Hopsten)
Vesting Holland South (Waalhoven/Moerdijk) – I./JG 26
(Bönninghardt), II./JG 27 (Wesel)

SECOND BOMBING WAVE

Moerdijk – IV.(St.)/LG 1 (Duisburg)
Moerdijk/Ockenburg/Waalhoven/Ypenburg – I./KG 30 (Oldenburg)
Rotterdam/Waalhoven – II./KG 30 (Oldenburg)

— First Bombing Wave
– – – First Fighter Wave – Strafing Missions
–·–·– First Fighter Wave – Escort/Patrol/Freie Jagd Missions
········ Second Bombing Wave

Aalborg

Faßberg

Delmenhorst

Oldenburg

Wangerooge

Marx

Gütersloh

Hopsten

GERMANY

Groningen

Leeuwarden

Dortmund

Gelsenkirchen-Buer

Kirchhellen

Essen-Mülheim

Wesel

Bönninghardt

Duisburg

Krefeld

THE NETHERLANDS

IJssel

Rhine

Waal

Maas (Meuse)

Bergen

De Vlijt

De Mok

De Kooy

Amsterdam

Schiphol

Utrecht

Valkenburg

Den Haag

Ypenburg

Ockenburg

Rotterdam

Waalhaven

Moerdijk

Gilze-Rijen

Welschop

Haamstede

BELGIUM

N

20 miles
20 km
0
0

Worried that the first bombing wave might not be able to effectively attack both the aircraft of the ML and the anti-aircraft defences of the airfields designated for later Luftlande operations, Putzier convinced Kesselring to temporarily give him the use of two Gruppen of Ju 88s from KG 30 for a second bombing wave, timed to strike roughly half an hour after the first bombing wave. The aim of the this second bombing wave was solely anti-aircraft and ground defence suppression around the drop zones for the 7.Fliegerdivision and the airfields assigned to the 22.Luftlande-Division. After the second wave of bombing was completed, transports of the Luftlandekorps would begin dropping elements of the 7.Fliegerdivision over both the Moerdijk-Rotterdam and Den Haag theatres of operation.

In addition to the bridges at Moerdijk, Dordrecht, and Rotterdam, the Fallschirmjäger were also tasked with capturing and securing the ML primary airfield at Waalhaven (*Landeplatz IV*) and three airfields outside of Den Haag: the auxiliary ML airfields at Valkenburg (*Landeplatz I*) and Ockenburg (*Landeplatz II*), and the ML primary airfield at Ypenburg (*Landeplatz III*). These four airfields would then be used to disembark the troops of the 22.Luftlande-Division. Luftlande troops landed at Waalhaven would assist the Fallschirmjäger in holding bridges into the Vesting Holland while the Luftlande troops landed at the airfields around Den Haag would move into the Dutch capital and capture the Dutch government, military high command, and the royal family – the Luftlande troops charged with the capture of the royal family were under personal orders from Hitler himself to observe strict royal protocols in this mission as well as to deliver a bouquet of flowers when meeting with Queen Wilhelmina.

At 1125hrs on 9 May, Heeresgruppe B received the following message from OKH: 'Gelb 10 Mai 1940, 05:35.' Shortly afterwards Luftflotte 2 received a similar message, authorizing Unternehmen F. At 2010hrs, Wehrmacht and Luftwaffe commanders received phone calls from OKH with the password 'Danzig', meaning the attack would proceed on schedule. It was at this time that the troops of the Luftlandekorps finally learned the true objective of the last several months of extensive training. The Fallschirmjäger had been conducting exercises against abandoned bunkers and fortifications along the old Czechoslovakian border as well as practising the capture of bridges across the Elbe but they had never been told the true purpose of these exercises. Neither had the Ju 52/3m pilots of the Luftlandekorps, who undertook training landings on sections of the Autobahn near Gütersloh throughout the spring of 1940; they were unaware that they had to be prepared to use straight sections of motorways as *ersatz* landing strips in the event they were unable to land on Dutch airfields. According to the planners of Fall Gelb, the element of surprise was of the utmost importance.

THE CAMPAIGN

Five costly days

Operations on 10 May 1940

Just after midnight[1] on Friday 10 May 1940, aircraft engines began turning over at airfields throughout north-west Germany and bomber crews were receiving last-minute mission updates. A little after 0100hrs, the He 111s and Ju 88s of KG 4 roared into the air and charted a north-westerly course, assembling into formations over the radio direction station at Friesoythe, just southwest of Oldenburg. The bombers then headed out into the North Sea near the German island of Juist, with some aircraft inadvertently passing into Dutch airspace over the provinces of Groningen and Drenthe. Once 15–20km offshore, KG 4's formations turned west and flew a course parallel to the Dutch coast, using Dutch lightships as directional markers. After rounding the West Frisian Islands and turning south into the English Channel, KG 4's Gruppen headed for the respective points at which they would turn inland. As KG 4's lead formations approached the point 20km to the west of the Maas estuary, the Geschwader commander, Oberst Martin Fiebig, noticed that these lead formations were proceeding ahead of schedule. Under orders not to head inland into Dutch airspace until 0350hrs, Fiebig signalled these aircraft to make a broad circle over the Channel to buy some time.

At roughly 0345hrs, all of his units had arrived at their waypoints to turn inland and at 0350hrs began the eastward approach to their targets. As KG 4's bombers were making their way off the Dutch coast, the Bf 109Ds of IV.(N)/JG 2 took off into the night sky. These

He 111 preparing for take-off in the pre-dawn darkness. (Author's collection)

1   On 10 May 1940, the Wehrmacht operated to *Mitteleuropäische Sommerzeit* (Central European Summer Time) or GMT/UTC+02:00, and all contemporary German sources list event times according to such. The Dutch armed forces operated according to *Amsterdamsche Tijd* (Amsterdam Time) or GMT/UTC+00:20; thus, event times in Dutch records are 01:40 behind times in German records. All times listed in this book are according to Amsterdamsche Tijd.

Dutch searchlight unit of the 3ᵉ Regiment Genietroepen, equipped with a listening device, observing and plotting the movement of unidentified aircraft in Dutch airspace. (Collectie Nederlands Instituut voor Militaire Historie)

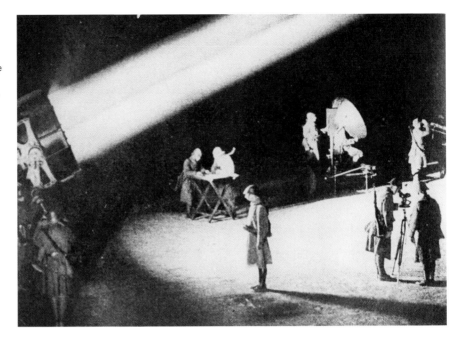

night fighters served as the navigational spearhead of Jagdfliegerführer 2's fighter umbrella; as dawn broke over western Germany, Bf 109E and Bf 110 day fighters took off and headed westward. ZG 1's Bf 110s flew directly to their targets while the Bf 109Es of JG 26 and JG 51 followed the Waal River and then spread out into their Frei Jagd patrol areas over Amsterdam and Rotterdam respectively.

The evening of 9–10 May was not a restful one for the Dutch however. Just after dark on 9 May a number of observation posts and border stations along the German border phoned the high command in Den Haag, reporting substantial activity. At 2315hrs, Generaal Best received a message from *Opperbevelhebber van Land- en Zeemacht*, or commander-in-chief, Henri Gerard Winkelman, ordering the Commando Luchtverdediging to be on full alert and ready for combat by 0300hrs. At 0100hrs on 10 May, Best relayed this message to his squadrons but advised them that take-offs could only occur on his orders or if hostile aircraft sightings were visually confirmed by the squadrons themselves. Beginning at 0136hrs, observer stations throughout the north-eastern areas of the Netherlands reported multi-engine aircraft flying overhead, headed toward the northwest with their navigation lights on. These overflights to the northwest continued until 0245hrs and the aircraft were likely identified as German bombers. The airfields inside the Vesting Holland received reports of these overflights shortly after they began and the base commander at Schiphol sounded the general alarm at 0200hrs, ordering aircraft be made ready for take-off and that anti-aircraft batteries and ground defences be manned.

The alarm soon spread to the other airfields and their squadrons and base defences were also manned. The fighter squadron commanders at both Bergen and De Kooy requested permission to send up small patrols to determine what the extensive aerial activity overhead was. The C.-Lvd. ordered them to stay on the ground and to await instructions; C-Lvd wondered if the Luftwaffe was conducting a large raid against Great Britain, given the direction the aircraft were heading and that they made no attempt to hide their movements by turning off their navigation lights. Reports of German overflights to the northwest ended shortly before 0300hrs and the skies over the Netherlands were again silent. Several squadrons maintained a state of readiness, expecting to be sent up on neutrality patrols once dawn arrived; some squadron commanders hoped for the opportunity to intercept the German bombers on their return flight if they happened again to pass through Dutch air space. Most squadron commanders felt a sense of unease about the scale of these German overflights; previous air space violations had largely been made by individual or small groups of aircraft. The Luftwaffe's ruse of flying towards Great Britain had caused some confusion among the ML's leadership but overall, the element of surprise was negated in that most ML squadrons maintained a degree of alert status.

At 0315hrs, the alarm sounded aboard the Dutch cruiser *Sumatra*, anchored in the roads off the port of Den Helder, as the sound of multi-engine aircraft was detected. A three-aircraft formation was observed heading south and, as it passed Den Helder, the aircraft dropped mines into the sea. Having identified the aircraft as German, *Sumatra*'s anti-aircraft batteries opened fire as additional aircraft approached, flying along the coast. This formation also was seen to drop mines in the water and then sped off, evading the anti-aircraft fire. Throughout the evening of 9–10 May, 20 Heinkel He 115 floatplanes from 3./Ku.Fl.Gr. 106, 3./Ku.Fl.Gr. 506, and 3./Ku.Fl.Gr. 906, and seven He 111H-4s of 1./KGr.126 flew several sorties in which they dropped around 100 *Luftminen B* (LMB) parachute mines off the Dutch and Belgian coasts. Once these mines landed in the water and floated back to the surface, a magnetic detonator was activated which would then go off if a ship passed within close proximity.

In Dutch waters aircraft laid mines in the Nieuwe Waterweg and off Den Helder, the Hoek van Holland, Ijmuiden, and Vlissingen. In a continuing effort to disrupt sea traffic between Great Britain and the Netherlands, the aircraft of the 9.Flieger-Division would lay magnetic mines off Dutch ports again on the evenings of 10–11 and 12–13 May. Overall, the effort put into these mining operations was not worth the tangible effect; only four ships were lost to magnetic mines in Dutch waters, only one, the 4,191-ton liner *Van Rensselaer*, being of any significance. Nevertheless, it was an attempt by the Luftwaffe to control the events of Unternehmen F on the sea as well as in the air and on the ground. *Sumatra* happened to observe some of the last sorties of what was the first offensive action in the German campaign against the Netherlands. These later minelaying flights were also observed on shore at Den Helder by naval personnel, alerted by *Sumatra*'s anti-aircraft fire, who noted that the last mines were dropped at around 0345hrs. The Koninklijke Marine's command was alerted but no immediate action was taken. There were still many questions as to what was actually going on but 10 minutes later that confusion would evaporate.

The cockpit of an He 111 from KG 4, with the navigator charting the aircraft's course over the North Sea. In an effort to obtain surprise, Putzier's first bombardment wave departed its bases in Germany and headed northward into the North Sea; it then headed westward around the Dutch coastline in order to approach its targets from the west, the direction German aircraft would least be expected from. (Collectie Nederlands Instituut voor Militaire Historie)

An He 111 of KGr 126 about to be loaded with two Luftminen B (LMB) parachute mines. In an effort to interdict shipping coming and going from Dutch ports, He 111s and He 115 floatplanes laid magnetic mines off the entrances to Dutch waterways throughout the Meidagen. (Author's collection)

Attack on Waalhaven

At 0350hrs, Oberst Fiebig led his *Stabskette* and the 18 He 111Ps of II./KG 4 low over the Dutch coastline at an altitude of 100m; all of KG 4's He 111 groups approached their targets at this low altitude in an attempt to avoid being spotted from a distance. Fiebig's navigator guided II./KG 4 up the Haringvliet estuary to the island of Tiengemeten, at which point the bombers set a course northward towards their target: the airfield at Waalhaven, located to the south-east of Rotterdam. The He 111s of II./KG 4 were each armed with 32 SC 50 (*Sprengbombe Cylindrisch*, or cylindrical explosive) general purpose 50kg bombs. Their objective was to neutralize the Dutch fighters based at Waalhaven as well as the anti-aircraft batteries around the airfield. The lower-calibre 50kg bombs were expected to accomplish this without causing heavy damage to the runway or tarmacs which were vital for the later Luftlande operation.

A German soldier, waving from the cockpit of the wreck of Fokker G.1A 302 of 3e JaVA at Waalhaven Airfield. 302 was destroyed at the beginning of the Luftwaffe's attack on the airfield by the Stabskette of KG 4. (Collectie Nederlands Instituut voor Militaire Historie)

On the ground at Waalhaven, the Fokker G.1 fighters of the *3e Jachtvliegtuigafdeeling* (3rd Fighter Squadron), or 3e JaVA, were dispersed around the airfield and the base's anti-aircraft batteries were manned. At 0130hrs, 3e JaVA's commander, Kapitein H.J. Scholtmeijer, was awakened with Generaal Best's alert command and ordered his ground crews to prepare the squadron's G.1s for take-off. At 0230hrs the mechanics were warming up the fighters' engines and their crews were assembling at the base command post. 0300hrs passed without orders from the C.-Lvd. but Scholtmeijer kept his crews on standby, given the numerous reports of airspace violations within the last hour and a half. Four of

The wreck of He 111 5J+DA of KG 4, Geschwaderkommodore Oberst Martin Fiebig's personal aircraft. The bomber was first damaged over Waalhaven by 1e Luitenant Piet Noomen in G.1A 312 and later finished off by 1e Luitenant Gerben Sonderman in G.1A 311. (Courtesy of the Douglas Dildy Collection)

the squadron's G.1s, 309, 311, 312, and 334, were parked on the tarmac adjacent to the civilian airport terminal, hangars, and the buildings of the Vliegtuigenfabriek Koolhoven, or Koolhoven Aircraft Factory. The remaining operational G.1s, 302, 315, 319, 328, 329, 330, and 335 were parked around the perimeter of the airfield's grass runway. A twelfth G.1, 316, was parked at the northwest corner of the airfield but was not combat-ready.

At 0355hrs, ground crew at the western edge of the airfield spotted a group of three aircraft coming in from the west at low altitude; initially the mechanics thought it was a patrol coming from the base at Ypenburg but instead it was Fiebig's Stabskette of KG 4. As they zoomed over the western perimeter of the airfield, the three Heinkels opened fire with their machine guns, strafing the southern side of the landing area and dropping their bombs. On this attack run a bomb hit between the tails of G.1 302, parked at the southwestern corner of the airfield, and the explosion blew the back of the aircraft upward with the front resting on its nose. Scholtmeijer ordered his pilots to immediately scramble as additional Heinkels were observed approaching from the west.

Scholtmeijer's adjutant, 1e Luitenant Aart van Oorschot, phoned the C.-Lvd., informing them of the attack but initially he was not believed; Scholtmeijer, overhearing this exchange, grabbed the phone and stuck the receiver out the window as the next passing group of Heinkels dropped their bombs. Only after hearing these explosions did the C.-Lvd. acknowledge that the attack was under way and that the Netherlands was now at war with Germany. Generaal Best issued a general scramble order to all of his squadrons but not all would receive the alert before other groups of Luftwaffe attackers struck their targets.

1e Luitenant Piet Noomen, in G.1A 312, was the first of 3e JaVA's pilots to take to the skies. As Noomen took off, a Kette of He 111s passed over, having turned around and made another attack from the east. Noomen pursued the three Heinkels and pushed his throttles to full. At a distance of 60m Noomen opened fire with his eight machine guns on the Heinkel in the centre of the formation, which happened to be Fiebig's aircraft; the fire raked across the Heinkel's fuselage and soon the bomber shuddered and dropped out of formation. The upper dorsal turret gunner in the He 111 to the left of Fiebig's opened fire on Noomen's G.1, holing the right wing. Noomen quickly turned his guns on the He 111 to the left of Fiebig's, knocking out the firing machine gun and hitting the left engine. Smoke erupted from the damaged engine and the bomber dropped away; this He 111 of Stab./KG 4 made its way back to its base at Fassberg. Shortly afterwards, Noomen's gunner signalled him to check his right wing and he quickly observed that the fuel tank had been punctured. He switched off the right engine to prevent the fuel tank from catching fire and headed back to the airfield

Fokker G.1A 312 stuck in soft soil in the north-west corner of Waalhaven Airfield after being flown in combat by 1ᵉ Luitenant Piet Noomen. (Courtesy of the Douglas Dildy Collection)

to make an immediate landing. Noomen touched down on the north-western part of the field where the terrain was rather swampy and was unable to taxi his aircraft back to the tarmac.

The second 3ᵉ JaVA pilot to get airborne was 1ᵉ Luitenant Jan Pieter Kuipers in G.1A 309, which was parked on an extension of the tarmac adjacent to the Koolhoven factory. 309's mechanics were able to immediately turn over its engines but just as Kuipers was about to taxi, a bomb from a passing He 111 struck the ground right between the aircraft's tails and wedged itself between the tail wheel and the ground. Fortunately, it did not explode. Having dived for cover and having caught their breath after their escape from certain death, Kuipers' ground crew lifted 309's tail over the bomb and the aircraft was able to get under way. Kuipers took off and shortly afterwards was able to position himself behind a Kette of Heinkels. At 200m Kuipers opened fire, sending one of the bombers down; this He 111, like 5J+DN of 5./KG 4 made a forced landing near Portugaal to the south-west of Rotterdam and Oberleutnant Roth and his crew were taken prisoner. Kuipers then caught up with another He 111 of 5./KG 4 over the oil refineries at Pernis and attacked it before having to head back to Waalhaven because of a damaged engine; He 111 5J+JN limped along for a while but eventually came down near Rosmalen to the south-west of Nijmegen. 309's left engine quit but Kuipers was able to bring it down for a hard landing at Waalhaven.

After taking off in G.1A 329, 1ᵉ Luitenant Karl Woudenberg observed a lone Ju 87 Stuka to the south of Waalhaven and attacked it. Almost simultaneously however, bullets went whizzing by and he turned to discover two Bf 109s on his tail. Woudenberg pulled up, went into a loop, and completed an Immelman turn; the Bf 109s flew past and did not pursue. Woudenberg then set a course back towards Waalhaven and several minutes later came upon a Kette of Ju 52/3ms from 12./KGzbV.1. After engaging the transports and shooting one down, Woudenberg disengaged and headed back for the airfield. On his return flight however, he was attacked by what he identified as a Bf 110. After using the G.1A's superior manoeuvrability to evade several high-speed attacks from the German aircraft, Woudenberg turned toward the German fighter as it was about to make another attack; opening fire before the German pilot, he scored several hits, sending the invader limping away. This aircraft which Woudenberg identified as a Bf 110 was most likely Ju 88A 4D+(?)H from 3./KG 30 which has been attributed to Woudenberg in several sources; it returned badly damaged to Munster and was written off. With his ammunition now almost completely expended and observing the smoke rising from Waalhaven, Woudenberg turned away from the combat area and searched for an alternate landing site. While flying near the coast Woudenberg spotted two G.1As parked on the beach near Oostvoorne. He safely landed alongside the two aircraft, piloted by 1ᵉ Luitenant Gerben Sonderman and Sergeant Herman Souffree[2].

Sergeant Herman Souffree got G.1A 328 into the air and quickly spotted a group of nine He 111s to the west, breaking off into their Ketten and preparing for an attack run on the airfield. Souffree flew around to the rear of a Kette and attacked, sweeping his guns across the bombers

2   For details about 1ᵉ Luitenant Gerben Sonderman's flight, see pp. 37

at first but then targeting the Kette leader; the He 111P, 5J+KN of 5./KG 4, began to smoke and dropped out of formation, eventually making a forced landing near Zevenbergschehoek. Just as Souffree watched the bomber slip away, bullets began to tear through the G.1; a number of Bf 109s had dropped in from above and were closing in for the kill. The Messerschmitts formed a rotating wheel around Souffree's more manoeuvrable G.1A, firing when the opportunity presented itself. Realizing he stood little chance in this circle of death, Souffree dived straight at one of the circling Bf 109s, startling the German pilots and breaking out of the wheel. It was not long before three of the fighters dove after him in pursuit. Souffree jerked up on his stick and entered a loop but once he reached its apex he eased back on the stick and maintained a horizontal course, upside down. The pursuing Bf 109s followed him into the loop but continued down through the apex, assuming that was the Dutchman's intention; Souffree now had the drop on his pursuers. He pulled back and righted his G.1, and fired at one of the Bf 109s. As Souffree headed back towards Waalhaven, G.1A 329 pulled up alongside Souffree and he saw Woudenberg making gestures to his landing gear. Souffree checked and found his landing gear was down. It turned out that enemy fire had damaged his hydraulic system and that his landing gear was extended while dogfighting with the Bf 109s. With the airfield still under attack, Souffree headed west to find somewhere safe to land and soon spotted the G.1A of 1ᵉ Luitenant Gerben Sonderman on a beach near Oostvoorne. Souffree brought his fighter in for a landing and shortly thereafter he was joined by Woudenberg.

Fokker G.1A 311 shooting down Bf 109D, Rotterdam, 0430hrs 10 May 1940

Shortly after the Heinkel He 111s of II./KG 4 began their attack against Waalhaven Airfield, 1ᵉ Luitenant Gerben Sonderman climbed into his G.1, 311, which was on the north-west corner of the tarmac. After his mechanics started its engines, Sonderman began taxiing as his gunner pulled out the chocks under the wheels; his gunner was still climbing into the cockpit when Sonderman applied full throttle and took off. Sonderman was arguably the most skilled pilot within 3ᵉ JaVA. He had served as the Fokker company's chief test pilot from 1938 until he was called up for military service in early 1940 and he was used to performing aerobatic manoeuvres in most of the Fokker aircraft employed by the ML and knew the limits to which he could push his G.1.

As Sonderman climbed, he observed a Ju 52 flying above him. Sonderman let loose a burst with his eight machine guns and the Ju 52 made an immediate evasive dive as the G.1 zoomed past the slow transport. Sonderman put his G.1 into a tight turn and he was quickly again on the transport's tail. A second gun burst sent the lumbering transport down; this Ju 52, no. 6404 from 9./KGzbV.I, made a forced landing near Heinenoord on the Oude Maas south of Rotterdam and its crew and 15 Fallschirmjäger from III./IR16 were taken prisoner. As Sonderman watched the Ju 52 go down, bullets tore through the G.1A's radio set as a Bf 109 flew past from above. Sonderman took evasive action and observed several Bf 109s to his rear; he had been bounced by the Bf 109Ds of 10.(N)/JG 2. The fighter that first attacked him was turning to get on the G.1's tail but Sonderman used the superior manoeuvrability of the G.1 to twist himself into a firing position on the German. A sweep of machine-gun fire damaged the Bf 109 which went down (the identity and fate of the aircraft is unknown). There were still other German fighters swarming around him and Sonderman continued to fly evasively, using his aerobatic skills to dance around the faster single-engine fighters. One of the Bf 109s made a wide turn and attempted a head-on attack against the G.1 but missed. Sonderman, having dodged the incoming fire, shot back before banking to avoid a head-on collision. His marksmanship was spot on; the Bf 109 was hit and was last seen diving toward the ground.

This Bf 109D, piloted by Feldwebel Peter Keller of 10.(N)/JG 2, made a forced landing south of Rotterdam and Keller was taken into captivity, eventually being sent to a POW camp in Canada. By this time Sonderman realized that his ammunition was low and disengaged from the remaining Bf 109s, heading west toward the sea. His hunt was not quite yet over however. As he approached the coast, Sonderman spotted an He 111 at low altitude heading east. Sonderman got behind the bomber and poured his remaining ammunition into it. Sonderman's final kill happened to be He 111 5J+DA, Oberst Martin Fiebig's aircraft; the bomber made a belly landing in a farm field and Fiebig and three of his crew were later taken prisoner for the duration of the Meidagen. Now out of ammunition, Sonderman felt it imperative to land and he observed a smooth stretch of beach below him that would make a suitable landing site. Sonderman landed G.1A 311 on a beach near Oostvoorne, where he was later joined by two of his comrades from 3ᵉ JaVA.

Fokker G.1A 328, flown by Sergeant Herman Souffree of 3ᵉ JaVA during the attack on Waalhaven Airfield. (Courtesy of the Douglas Dildy Collection)

Back at Waalhaven, 2ᵉ Luitenant Han van der Jagt ran towards his G.1A 334 but as he approached it a bomb from a passing He 111 struck the left side of the aircraft; the explosion destroyed the left wing and tail and killed van der Jagt's gunner, who had run to the aircraft ahead of him. Van der Jagt then ran back to the command post and requested to take up another aircraft. Kapitein Scholtmeijer told him to take up the squadron's reserve aircraft, G.1 319, which was at the far western end of the airfield. Dodging German strafing runs, van der Jagt slowly made the long trek across the airfield to 319. After the engines were started, van der Jagt realized that 319's gunner was nowhere to be found but decided to take off anyway. He barrelled down the airfield in an eastward direction, lifting off the ground just before the tarmac and clearing the burning Koolhoven hangars with just feet to spare.

The details of van der Jagt's sortie after take-off are not exactly known. Witnesses on the ground at Hoeksche Waard observed two G.1As attacking a flight of German bombers, and then later dogfighting with Bf 109 fighters. This combat was later confirmed by Sergeant Major Jan Buwalda in G.1 330, which happened to be one of the two G.1s involved. Witnesses on the ground in Vlaardingen later observed a G.1A attacking several Ju 52/3ms, which also received defensive fire from the upper gun positions on the transports. The left engine of the G.1A was hit and suddenly burst into flames; the fighter rolled over to the left and dived, eventually crashing into the Nieuwe Maas. Van der Jagt was listed as missing in action until 20 June 1940, when his body washed up on the shore near Vlaardingen. It is not known if van der Jagt succeeding in shooting down any enemy aircraft but he was the only pilot of 3ᵉ JaVA to lose his life on 10 May.

1ᵉ Luitenant Aart van Oorschot ran to his personal car and drove across the field at Waalhaven to G.1A 315, which was parked on the southern end of the airfield to the right of the destroyed G.1 302. Van Oorschot took off and spotted an He 111 preparing for an attack run on the airfield. Closing on the invader, he fired on the bomber in a head-on attack and looked back to see the damaged aircraft drop its payload over the pastures south of the airfield and then turn to the east. Van Oorschot turned to pursue the damaged bomber but found that, due to the earlier damage to the aircraft's wing and tail, his maximum speed was limited to around 400km/h. He persisted in the chase however and caught up to his prey near Arnhem. Under standing orders not to cross the German border, Van Oorschot turned around and set a course back to Waalhaven as the German bomber made a fortuitous escape.

As he flew to the southwest, Van Oorschot spotted a large formation of Ju 52/3ms to the south of Dordrecht. He positioned himself behind a Kette of three transports, pumping bullets into the fuselages of all three aircraft. Surprisingly the aircraft did not seem to be seriously damaged so he fired into them several more times, but again it appeared to have no effect; one of the Ju 52/3ms, no. 6403 from 9./KGzbV.1, later made a forced landing at Waalhaven and was attributed to Van Oorschot as a kill. By this time Van Oorschot was low on ammunition and, after observing a number of Ju 52/3ms on the ground at Waalhaven and a fire fight between the airfield's garrison and German infantry, he aborted to the airfield at De Kooy. Upon landing, his G.1A ran into a barbed wire obstruction which became entangled around the right propeller and brought the aircraft to an abrupt stop. 315 required repairs but at least Van Oorschot made it safely back to the ground.

Sergeant Major Jan Buwalda was the last of 3^e JaVA's pilots to take off during the initial German attack on Waalhaven. His mechanics had difficulty turning over his aircraft's engines but eventually he got G.1A 330 into the air. After freeing van der Jagt up from several pursuing Bf 109s, Buwalda came across He 111P-2 5J+ST of 2./KG 4 flying to the southeast over Nieuw-Beijerland, to the southwest of Rotterdam. Buwalda pursued the bomber and fired several bursts into it; one of its engines was hit and sputtered out, compelling its pilot to make a forced landing near Goudszwaard. After this pursuit, Buwalda decided to head back towards Waalhaven but soon encountered another lone German bomber. Do 17Z QU+KH of Aufkl.St.(F)/7.Fl.Div. was on its way to Waalhaven on a photographic reconnaissance mission when Buwalda swept in from behind and knocked out one of its engines with two short eight-gun bursts. The Do 17 dived down and made a belly landing near Cillaarshoek, to the west of Dordrecht. Buwalda was feeling quite satisfied with his work when he heard his gunner opening fire behind him; several Bf 109Ds of IV.(N)/JG 2 and Bf 109Es of III./JG 26

Six of the pilots of 3e JaVA who defended the skies over Waalhaven during the Luftwaffe's initial assault on the morning of 10 May. Clockwise, staring in the upper left corner: 1^e Luitenant Piet Noomen (G.1A 312), 1^e Luitenant Jan Pieter Kuipers (309), 1^e Luitenant Karl Woudenberg (329), Sergeant Major Jan Buwalda (330), 1^e Luitenant Aart van Oorschot (315), and Sergeant Herman Souffree (328). (Collectie Nederlands Instituut voor Militaire Historie)

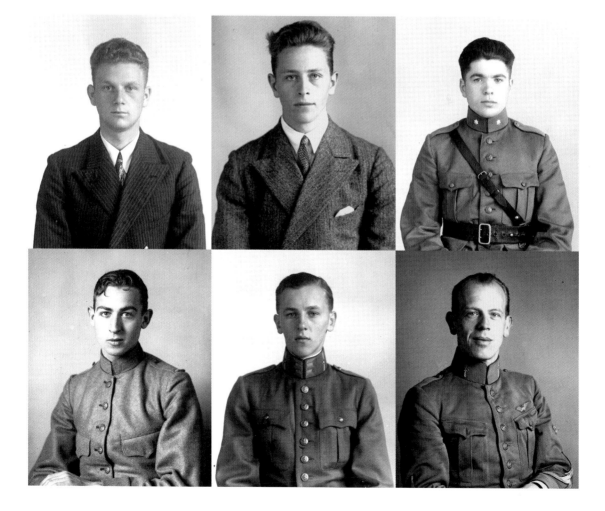

OPPOSITE ATTACKS AGAINST DUTCH AIRFIELDS BY FLIEGERKORPS ZBV.2, 0355–0445HRS, 10 MAY 1940

If the waves of Ju 52 transports carrying General Student's Fallschirmjäger were to undertake their paradrops without interference from the fighter squadrons of the Dutch ML, air superiority over the drop zones had to be achieved effectively and quickly. To this end, Generalmajor Richard Putzier assigned the 59 He 111s and 21 Ju 88s of KG 4, as well as 12 He 111s from KGr 126 to bombardment missions against the ML's airfields at the outset of Unternehmen F. In the Polish Campaign, the Heinkel He 111 had demonstrated its ability to make accurate horizontal bombing attacks against airfields at low to medium altitudes. As there were only a few Ju 88s operational, these versatile aircraft were reserved for making precision dive-bombing attacks against specific targets such as aircraft hangars or anti-aircraft batteries. Once the He 111s and Ju 88s began the approach to their targets from the sea, they dropped to an altitude of 30m in an effort to avoid detection. After passing over the Dutch coast, the Ju 88s broke away from the He 111s and began a climb to 3,000m, the minimum altitude for a dive-bombing attack. Once over an airfield, Ju 88s commenced a 50° dive against their target and released their bombs at 1,500m, after which their elevators automatically moved into the full-up position.

Each Ju 88 carried two SC (*Sprengbombe Cylindrisch* or cylindrical explosive) 500 general-purpose 500kg bombs, each bomb intended to cause maximum damage to a specific target. The He 111s made their horizontal bombing runs at an altitude of 100m; gunners in the bombers took advantage of steady approach to strafe targets of opportunity. Each He 111 carried up to 32 SC 50 general-purpose 50kg bombs, which when dropped in a swathe caused extensive damage against spread-out light targets such as parked aircraft, tarmacs, or runways. After releasing their bombs, the bombers made strafing attacks before returning to their bases. Putzier's bombers also had suppression support from several units of Bf 110s Generalmajor Kurt-Bertram von Döring's Jagdfliegerführer 2; these heavy fighters were tasked with strafing missions against nine Dutch airfields, commencing shortly after the initial bombardment attacks. This combination of horizontal bombardment, dive-bombing, and strafing attacks in theory would effectively cripple the ML on the ground at the outset of the campaign; if surprise was achieved.

had observed him shoot down the Do 17 and were now out for revenge. Buwalda took evasive action and headed to the south, his gunner firing accurately and hitting several of the German fighters. One of these damaged Bf 109s was later written off when it returned to base. Several of the Bf 109s broke off the fight but two from IV.(N)/JG 2 persisted and eventually damaged 330's engines. In the fight, Buwalda's gunner also accidently hit the tail stabilizer and after this Buwalda had no choice but to make an emergency landing. He brought 330 in for a wheels-up landing in a field near Zevenbergen, just to the south of Moerdijk. Oberfeldwebel Hermann Förster of IV.(N).JG 2 was credited with the kill. Buwalda and his gunner commandeered a nearby car and attempted to drive back to Waalhaven.

The pilots of 3e JaVA fought exceptionally well, given the amount of enemy fighter activity, in the skies over the Rotterdam area; together they achieved 11 confirmed kills (5× He 111s, 1× Ju 88, 1× Do 17, 1× Bf 109, and 3× Ju 52/3ms) along with several further claims, while only one of their number was shot down (van der Jagt) and one had to make a forced landing (Buwalda). Within an hour of the beginning of the bombardment of Waalhaven, most of the airfield's buildings were in flames or severely damaged. Fiebig's Kette targeted the airport's buildings and the Koolhoven factory complex and succeeded in destroying them on its attack runs. Fiebig's other Ketten were under strict orders not to drop any bombs on the field itself as it was needed later for Ju 52/3m landings. Instead, they targeted anti-aircraft batteries and infantry positions around the perimeter of the airfield.

Around 0430hrs, Ju 88s of II./KG 30 arrived overhead and also targeted Waalhaven's anti-aircraft batteries and others in the Rotterdam area. One of 5./KG 30's pilots on this mission was Leutnant Werner Baumbach, who would go on to destroy 300,000 tons of Allied shipping and later became the commander of Kampfgeschwader 200, the Luftwaffe's secretive special operations unit. While over Waalhaven, Baumbach was attacked by a G.1 (identity unknown) but was saved by the timely intervention of a Bf 109. The ground defences at Waalhaven took a heavy beating and were in a state of confusion when Fallschirmjäger began to rain down around the airfield roughly an hour after the initial attack.

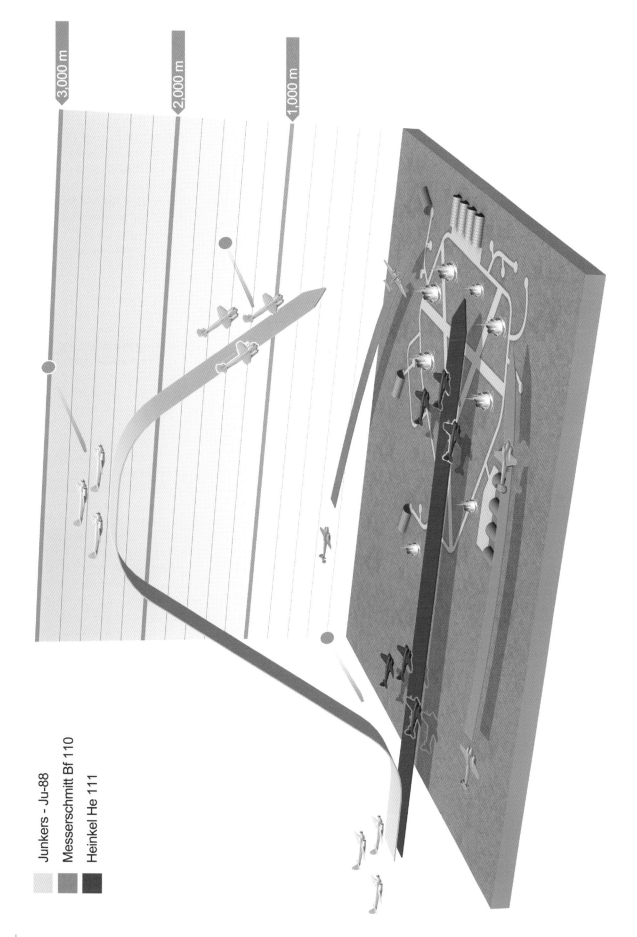

Junkers - Ju-88

Messerschmitt Bf 110

Heinkel He 111

3,000 m

2,000 m

1,000 m

Attack on Ypenburg

At around 0355hrs, the He 111s of 1./KG 4 crossed the Dutch coastline near the Hoek van Holland, headed for Ypenburg Airfield which was located just east of The Hague. On the ground at Ypenburg, the two squadrons of the Jachtgroep Veldleger had been on standby since Generaal Best's initial alert at 0100hrs. Initially only the 1ᵉ Afdeling van de Jachtgroep Veldleger (1-V-2) had been stationed at Ypenburg but it was joined by the 3ᵉ Afdeling van de Jachtgroep Veldleger (3-V-2) on 7 May. 3-V-2 had been stationed at Soesterberg as a tactical ground strike squadron assigned to the army but was reassigned to the C.-Lvd. as an air defence squadron as the fear of war increased. The Douglas DB-8A/3N was certainly no fighter but the C.-Lvd. was desperate for any available aircraft. There was one other squadron present at Ypenburg that morning, the IIᵉ Verkenningsgroep with its seven operational C.Vs and five operational FK 51s. These aircraft were moved outside of the airfield by their ground crews and camouflaged. At 0200hrs the ground crews of 1-V-2 moved Fokker D.XXIs 212, 215, 216, 217, 222, 227, 228, 246 and 247 out of the hangars and parked them in a line along the north-western edge of the airfield. The ground crews of 3-V-2 moved its 11 Douglas DB-8A/3Ns into a line along the southwestern edge of the airfield. Mechanics warmed up the aircraft engines while the aircrews had a quick breakfast. By 0300hrs, the aircrews were at their aircraft and remained there on standby. They were still there when at 0400hrs in the distance to the northwest, three twin-engine aircraft were spotted, approaching fast and at low altitude; it was the lead Kette of 1./KG 4, commanded by Oberstleutnant Hans-Joachim Rath.

The alarm sounded as soon as the three He 111s were spotted and the engines of all of the parked aircraft were immediately turned over as 1-V-2's and 3-V-2's mechanics were still on standby. As 1-V-2's D.XXIs were in a long, single line, each aircraft was able to take off as soon as its pilot was ready; some were even off the ground before the first German bombs were dropped. As the D.XXIs climbed, their pilots had just enough time to form into their three patrols before a new group of attackers arrived on the scene; coming in from the east shortly after the bombardment began were 22 Bf 110C fighters of II./ZG 1. The Zerstörers dived on the ascending D.XXIs and within moments a giant mêlée began over the airfield. 1ᵉ Luitenant Pierre Ruijs de Perez, commander of 1-V-2's first three-plane patrol, in D.XXI 222 initially ignored the Bf 110s and went after the He 111s. He manoeuvred into a position behind one of the bombers and pressed the trigger; click… nothing. The loading mechanism for his machine guns malfunctioned and there was nothing he could do about it while airborne. He broke away from the bombers, found his wingman, Sergeant Guus

Fokker D.XXIs of the 1ᵉ Afdeling van de Jachtgroep Veldleger (1-V-2) lined up at Ypenburg Airfield. D.XXIs 215 and 216 are identifiable, which were, respectively, piloted by 2ᵉ Luitenant Govert Steen and Sergeant Guus Kiel on the morning of 10 May. (Collectie Nederlands Instituut voor Militaire Historie)

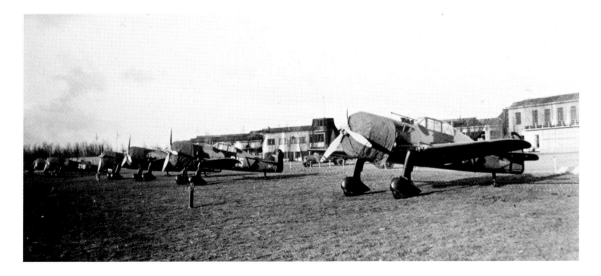

Kiel in D.XXI 216, and signalled his predicament. Ruijs de Perez signalled Kiel to take over command of the patrol but Ruijs de Perez did not leave the fight. He remained with his patrol for some time, having decided to serve as an extra pair of eyes for his wingmen.

Given the larger number of German fighters present, Ruijs de Perez's formation was not able to stay together indefinitely and Sgt. Kiel and Ruijs de Perez's other wingman, Sergeant Jaap Eden in D.XXI 247, eventually broke away into their own dogfights. At this point, Ruijs de Perez decided it was time to land and headed to the west to find a location where he could safely touch down. Before long however some pursuing Bf 110s caught up with him and attacked. Ruijs de Perez was wounded in his upper arm and 222 was seriously damaged. Around 0435hrs, Ruijs de Perez managed to bring his aircraft down near the village of Monster, to the southwest of Den Haag, and made a rough landing, further damaging 222; the aircraft was a write-off and Ruijs de Perez was taken to a hospital.

Wreck of Fokker D.XXI 222, flown by 1ᵉ Luitenant Pierre Ruijs de Perez of 1-V-2 on the morning of 10 May. 222's machine guns malfunctioned during the battle over Ypenburg but Ruijs de Perez remained airborne, drawing fire away from his wingmen until eventually shot down by Bf 110s. (Collectie Nederlands Instituut voor Militaire Historie)

Sergeant Kiel in 216 also went after the He 111s but was unable to shoot any down as he frequently had to evade attacks from the Bf 110s. After losing contact with his wingman, Kiel happened upon a group of Ju 52/3ms from I./KGrzbV.12, headed for Ypenburg, and attacked; one of the Ju 52/3ms he targeted caught fire and was seen to dive away. By this time Kiel had been in the air for roughly an hour and was low on both ammunition and fuel. He landed at Ruigenhoek at around 0515hrs where 216 was refuelled and rearmed. 216's machine guns had jammed however and there was no compressed air at Ruigenhoek for the aircraft's pneumatic loading system so Kiel decided to take off for another airfield where his aircraft could receive the necessary maintenance. As he approached Ypenburg he could see large clouds of smoke rising above the airfield's damaged buildings so he turned north towards the airfield at Valkenburg, hoping it had not been subjected to attack.

Shortly thereafter he was intercepted by five Bf 110s of 2./ZG 1. There was little Kiel could do as his machine guns were not operational; despite intense evasive manoeuvres there were just too many of the enemy. Eventually wounded and with 216's rudder shot to pieces, Kiel brought 216 down for a crash landing outside of Den Deyl, to the southwest of Leiden; Feldwebel Erich Puschnerus of 2./ZG 1 was credited with the kill. Kiel survived the landing but stayed in the cockpit of his destroyed aircraft for four hours before seeking medical assistance due to nearby ground combat.

Kiel's wingman, Sgt. Eden in 247, had a bit more luck in the air than his comrades. Eden engaged the Bf 110s over Ypenburg, using his D.XXI's superior manoeuvrability to outturn the faster yet bulkier Zerstörers. Eventually Eden got on the tail of a Bf 110C of 4./ZG 1, piloted by Unteroffizier Helmut Voss. Eden skilfully hit both the Zerstörer's engines; Voss managed to limp his damaged aircraft out of the combat area but was finally forced to make a belly landing far to the south near Vlissingen. By around 0500hrs, 247 was low on ammunition, and when Eden touched down at Ypenburg, his good fortune quickly ended. Eden's landing was observed in the air by Oberleutnant Victor Mölders (younger brother of the famous Luftwaffe ace Werner Mölders) of 2./ZG 1, who then dived for an attack run. Mölders strafed 247 just after Eden had left the cockpit, setting the aircraft on fire. Eden then ran towards D.XXI 227 which was still sitting in front of the hangars; 227 was operational but its armament had been removed for routine maintenance. Before Eden even reached the aircraft, Mölders attacked it in another strafing pass; 227 caught fire and was likewise burnt out.

The commander of 1-V-2's second patrol, 2ᵉ Luitenant Govert Steen, suffered from the same misfortune as Ruijs de Perez. After taking off in D.XXI 246, Steen went to test his machine guns; just like Ruijs de Perez, click… nothing. Steen's wingmen, Sergeant Jan Linzel in D.XXI 215 and 2ᵉ Luitenant Arnoldus van de Vaart in D.XXI 212, were alongside him in formation at the time and he attempted to signal them about the malfunction. Linzel and van de Vaart misunderstood Steen's gestures and followed their patrol commander back to the ground at Ypenburg.

Amidst the chaos of the German attack, the three D.XXIs landed together on the airfield. Steen quickly informed the ground crew about his machine guns and ordered Linzel to switch planes with him. After only three minutes on the ground and with bombs falling around them, Steen and van de Vaart again took off. Linzel was not on the ground for long either. To their frustration, the attending mechanics found that the valves of the compressed air canisters for 246's loading system had not been opened during the morning's initial flight check. With this quickly remedied, Linzel too was quickly airborne. Steen and his wingmen were all quickly engaged in the mêlée over Ypenburg. Steen was involved in several dogfights but did not manage to score a kill. Around 0500hrs he was low on both ammunition and fuel and after determining that it was no longer safe to land at Ypenburg, he landed 215 on the beach at Kijkduin, directly west of Den Haag. 215 was later strafed there by German fighters and burned out.

Linzel made his way through the swarm of Bf 110s over Ypenburg and caught up with the He 111's of 1./KG 4 as they were forming up for the return flight to Gütersloh. He was firing on one of the bombers when he himself was pounced upon by a Bf 110. Linzel received a wound to his right thigh and 246 was heavily damaged. Losing consciousness, Linzel bailed out over Delft and safely reached the ground; he was rushed to hospital shortly thereafter. 246 crashed near Pijnacker, just east of Delft.

Messerschmitt Bf 110s of II./ZG 1 over the skies of Western Europe in the spring of 1940. During the assault on Ypenburg Airfield, II./ZG 1 was tasked with protecting the bombers of 1./KG 4, engaging any Dutch fighters over the airfield, and strafing targets of opportunity on the ground. (Author's collection)

Luitenant van de Vaart was the only pilot of his patrol to have any success that morning. As with Steen, he too was engaged in a number of dogfights over Ypenburg but was also unable to shoot down any of the attackers. Low on fuel, he decided to head for Schiphol around 0500hrs after observing the mess on the ground at Ypenburg. North of Leiden van de Vaart came upon a Dornier Do 215B-4 of 2./Aufkl.Gr.Ob.d.L., on a reconnaissance flight. Although low on ammunition, van de Vaart swept in behind the Do 215 and fired his remaining rounds into it; the Do 215 caught fire and its crew bailed out. In this brief fight however, the Do 215's rear gunner hit 212 in the engine, causing it to seize and then stop. With great skill van de Vaart glided his damaged fighter safely onto the field at Schiphol, where 212 would be repaired to fight another day.

The third patrol of 1-V-2, composed of 2ᵉ Luitenant F.G.B. Droste in D.XXI 228 and Sergeant P.J. Aarts in D.XXI 217, had better luck than the other patrols during the battle of Ypenburg. Both Droste and Aarts stayed together during their sortie. The pilots manoeuvred free from the swarm of Bf 110s over Ypenburg and eventually came across Ju 88s of I./KG 30 and II./KG 30, which were on anti-aircraft suppression missions over the Den Haag and Rotterdam areas. Over Den Haag Droste caught up with Ju 88A 4D+AM of 4./KG 30, piloted by Oberleutnant Theodor Beermann, and badly damaged it; one of its crew was killed in the air while Beermann and the remainder bailed out, with the aircraft crashing near Den Hoorn.

Another Ju 88A, 4D+FT of 1./KG 30 piloted by Oberleutnant W. Wülknitz, was attacked over Waalhaven around the same time by a single-engine fighter. Wülknitz was forced to bring his aircraft in for a belly landing near Zevenhuizen, to the northeast of Rotterdam. Some English-language sources claim that this Ju 88 was accidentally shot down by a Bf 109, but German sources attribute this kill to a D.XXI. While Droste or Aarts have not been traditionally credited with this kill, it appears that it could be attributed to one of them as 228 and 217 were the only D.XXIs in that general area at the time (some Dutch sources attribute a Bf 110 kill to Aarts but German sources list no Bf 110 being lost in the vicinity at the time; this kill may have been Ju 88 4D+FT). Droste eventually ran out of ammunition in his combat with the Ju 88s and then, with Aarts accompanying him, searched for a safe place to land. Around 0445hrs, they touched down at the auxiliary airfield at Ockenburg. Unfortunately, there was no fuel there and the pilots were unable to take off again.

Fokker D.XXI 228 (left) flown by 2ᵉ Luitenant F.G.B. Droste of 1-V-2 over Ypenburg on 10 May. Droste shot down Ju 88A 4D+AM of 4./KG 30 and, after running out of ammunition, later landed at Ockenburg where 228 was damaged later that morning in the ground battle for the airfield. (aircraft – Courtesy of the Douglas Dildy Collection; Droste – Collectie Nederlands Instituut voor Militaire Historie)

Wreck of Ju 88A 4D+FT, of 1./KG 30, near Zevenhuizen, likely shot down by either 2e Luitenant F.G.B. Droste or Sergeant P.J. Aarts of 1-V-2. (Collectie Nederlands Instituut voor Militaire Historie)

The two squadrons of the Jachtgroep Veldleger suffered catastrophic losses during the attack on Ypenburg. The 11 DB-8A/3Ns of 3-V-2 took off after the D.XXIs and engaged the attackers but the result was a quick and largely inevitable massacre. Seven were shot down, two made forced landings, and two safely landed at Ockenburg after running out of ammunition; eight of 3-V-2's aircrews were killed and its pilots did not achieve any confirmed kills. The heavy DB-8A/3N losses were unfortunate proof that the unwieldy light bomber had no business attempting to serve as a fighter. Of the eight D.XXIs of 1-V-2 that took off that morning, three were shot down, two were destroyed on the ground after landing, and three safely landed at Schiphol and Ockenburg.

Fortunately, none of 1-V-2's pilots were killed and they did achieve three confirmed kills and one probable. While the D.XXIs were certainly more manoeuvrable that the Bf 110s, of all the Dutch squadrons engaged that morning they had to face the largest concentration of German fighters due to Ypenburg being the specific target of II./ZG 1. Not only did the fighters of 1-V-2 have to contend with the 22 Bf 110s of II./ZG 1, but also the Bf 110s of 1./ZG 1 and 2./ZG 1 which were on Freie Jagd missions over the Den Haag and Rotterdam areas. On the ground however, the damage sustained by Ypenburg's anti-aircraft batteries and defensive positions was relatively light. Midway into the initial attack on Ypenburg, several Ju 88s of I./KG 30 attacked the airfield's defences but it was not as heavy an attack as that of II./KG 30 at Waalhaven.

The Douglas DB-8A/3Ns of the 3e Afdeling van de Jachtgroep Veldleger (3-V-2) at Soesterberg Airfield in March 1940. Stationed at Ypenburg on 10 May, these light bombers were sent up as fighters and suffered heavy losses. Only two out of the 11 DB-8A/3Ns that engaged the attackers landed safely after the battle over the airfield. (Courtesy of the Douglas Dildy Collection)

Attack on Schiphol

Around 0330hrs at Schiphol Airport outside of Amsterdam, the commander of 2ᵉ JaVA, Kapitein P.J.E. Janssens, told his pilots to stand down since a general alarm had still not been given by the ML command. 2ᵉ JaVA's D.XXI fighters had been taxied to the north-eastern edge of Schiphol's main runway and had been idling there since 0215hrs; around 0315hrs 2ᵉ JaVA's pilots switched off their engines and walked to the maintenance hangars at the southern end of the airport for some coffee. Between 0230hrs and 0300hrs the operational T.V bombers of BomVA were taxied from their dispersal positions along the Haagweg highway, located north of the airfield, to the north-eastern end of the runway and parked just to the left of 2ᵉ JaVA's fighters. BomVA's aircrews remained by their aircraft, reviewing their patrol orders, when 2ᵉ JaVA's pilots left their fighters. Schiphol's anti-aircraft batteries also remained on alert when 2ᵉ JaVA stood down.

At 0358hrs, just as the fighter pilots were sitting down to their coffee, three aircraft were observed approaching from the northwest at a height of just below 30m, Kapitein Janssens sounded the general alarm and ordered his pilots to scramble. As the pilots made the lengthy run from the hangars to the north-eastern end of the main runway three Heinkel He 111Ps of III./KG 4 sped by overhead and dropped their bombs on the barracks just northeast of the airport terminal building. Further He 111s swept in and made low-level attacks while 12 Ju 88As from 8. And 9./KG 4 arrived overhead and began making individual dive-bombing attacks against the hangars located along the south-eastern side of the airport and other targets of opportunity. As the bombers pounded the airbase, Bf 109Es from II./JG 26 came in at low level from the east and strafed ground targets between the bombing runs. Despite the surprise of the attack, all of D-XXI fighters of 2ᵉ JaVA made it into the air.

As the attack continued, 2ᵉ JaVA's D.XXIs climbed in an attempt to get above the German bombers. Normally the nine fighters of the 2ᵉ JaVA would have formed into patrols of three aircraft but coordination on this hectic morning was impossible; the squadron's radio truck, which relayed orders to the patrol commanders was knocked out of action during the bombardment. Not all D.XXIs were equipped with radios; only those of the patrol commanders who then communicated with their wingmen via hand signals. 2ᵉ JaVA's pilots were thus forced to take individual actions against the attackers, their only orders being to remain within a 25km radius of their airfield.

Fokker D.XXI 225 engaging Ju 88 5J+GT over Schiphol, 10 May 1940

One of the first Dutchmen engaged in combat, 1ᵉ Luitenant Nicolaas Sluyter in D.XXI no. 225, achieved the only success for the squadron in this engagement, shortly after 0400hrs. He was able to sweep in behind Ju 88 5J+GT of 9./KG 4 and rake the bomber with 7.7mm machine-gun fire, killing one of the gunners and causing the badly damaged aircraft to make a forced landing northwest of Schiphol. Sluyter had expended his ammunition in the fight with the Ju 88 and, after observing the ongoing bombardment and damage to Schiphol, decided to land at the small auxiliary airfield near the village of Ruigenhoek, ten miles to the west of Schiphol. Sluyter touched down there at 0415hrs and was surprised to find that the airfield's commander was not even aware that the country was under attack.

Sluyter then contacted Kapitein Janssens at Schiphol for orders but was told to stay put for the time being. Janssens, reasoning that Ruigenhoek was likely safe from German attack, decided to divert as many of his aircraft as possible there for further operations. Although Sluyter obtained the only kill for 2ᵉ JaVA in the skies over Schiphol, Dutch anti-aircraft fire around the airfield's perimeter proved to be very accurate and three of the attackers were claimed by flak during the bombardment. He 111 5J+PR of 7./KG 4 made a forced landing while Ju 88s 5J+AT and 5J+IT of 9./KG 4 both crashed into nearby waters. As the remaining bombers made their return trip to Delmenhorst, a Ju 88 of 8./KG 4 was mistakenly attacked by German anti-aircraft batteries near the Dutch border and made a forced landing just within German territory. These were relatively heavy losses for the Luftwaffe and no further bombing attacks were made against Schiphol during the invasion of the Netherlands.

Fokker D.XXIs and Fokker T.Vs photographed from the air at Schiphol prior to Dutch mobilization in August 1939. (Courtesy of the Aviation Museum Aviodrome, Netherlands)

Civilians examining Fokker D.XXI 245, flown by Sergeant Hein Bulten of 2ᵉ JaVA during the Luftwaffe's assault on Schiphol, which made an emergency landing near the village of Zwaagdijk. (Collectie Nederlands Instituut voor Militaire Historie)

Sergeant Ben de Geus in D.XXI 236 circled the airfield and engaged a Ju 88, knocking out its nose gun. Sergeant Frans Looyen in 229 fired at several aircraft, achieving no kills and was soon out of ammunition. Looyen spotted de Geus and pulled up alongside, signalling no ammo. De Geus acknowledged and escorted Looyen to the airfield at Ruigenhoek, near the coast north of Leiden, where 229 landed at 0430hrs. Ruigenhoek's airfield was constructed after the outbreak of war the previous autumn and in April it became the home of the reconnaissance aircraft of the 3ᵉ Verkenningsgroep. Ruigenhoek's runway was painted with dark lines so it resembled nearby farm meadows from the air and its aircraft were covered with camouflage netting; due to these measures, the Luftwaffe was not aware of its existence. In the distance de Geus spotted an He 111 and gave pursuit, firing his remaining rounds at the bomber until he too ran out of ammo and then landed at Ruigenhoek at 0435hrs. Ruigenhoek Airfield would go on to play a pivotal role for the ML throughout the rest of the campaign. Back over Schiphol, Sergeant Hein Bulten in 245 locked in combat with a Bf 109 from II./JG 26 but his fighter sustained damage that forced him to make an emergency landing near the village of Zwaagdijk; unable to be repaired there, D.XXI 245 was camouflaged and left where it landed.

2ᵉ Luitenant Hans Plesman, the son of KLM's Director Albert Plesman, in D.XXI 235 was perhaps the most fortunate of 2ᵉ JaVA's pilots over Schiphol. After being the last to take off, Plesman found himself alone over the airfield when seven Bf 109s of II./JG 26, passing overhead, spotted him and dived to attack. After their initial passes the German fighters formed a circle around the lone Dutchman like a pack of hungry wolves. Plesman instantly decided to engage one of the circling Bf 109s, emptying his guns at the fighter before using his aircraft's superior manoeuvrability to disengage. He came down at Schiphol at 0425hrs and upon inspection found 36 bullet holes in his aircraft.

1ᵉ Luitenant Antoine Bodaan in D.XXI 238 attempted to engage several of the attackers but came down empty handed at 0435hrs. Unwilling to give up quite yet, Bodaan bellowed from his cockpit for ground crew to refuel and rearm his aircraft. In spite of the ongoing bombardment, his aircraft was quickly readied and he roared back into the air at 0448hrs. He returned to Schiphol at 0535hrs, his ammunition again expended, and insisted upon another immediate return to the battle.

Of the remaining 2ᵉ JaVA pilots, Sergeants Jacobus 'Koos' Roos in D.XXI 239 and Gé Burger in D.XXI 213 both landed back at Schiphol, out of ammo, at 0418hrs and 0420hrs respectively, and 2ᵉ Luitenant Henk Sitter in D.XXI 224 touched down at 0445hrs. Of the D.XXIs that returned to Schiphol after this initial air battle, 213 and 239 required no repairs

Pilots of 2ᵉ JaVA in front of Fokker D.XXI 233, photographed during the winter of 1940; from left to right: 1ᵉ Luitenant Franciscus Bik, 2ᵉ Luitenant Hans Plesman, Sergeant Jacob van Zuijlen, Sergeant Gé Burger, and Sergeant Ben de Geus. (Courtesy of the Douglas Dildy Collection)

and Kapitein Janssens dispatched Plesman and Roos in them to Ruigenhoek to join Sluyter, Looyen, and de Geus. Despite being surprised and engaging in a hectic and uncoordinated aerial battle, all but one of 2ᵉ JaVA's fighters survived the initial German onslaught.

After Plesman and Roos arrived at Ruigenhoek in D.XXIs 231 and 239, they were ordered to join de Geus, Sluyter, and Looyen, in 224, 225, and 229 respectively, in a five-aircraft patrol over the area between Den Haag and Schiphol. To the west of Gouda, they came up on a lone Ju 52/3m from 3./KGzbV 9, which was on a return flight after disembarking Luftlande troops at Ockenburg. Defensive fire from the transport wounded Sluyter in one of his arms but the remaining D.XXIs attacked, with Plesman delivering the *coup de grace*. After this encounter, the patrol headed back to the west, with Sluyter and de Geus landing at Schiphol and Plesman and Roos returning to Ruigenhoek. After the attack on the Ju 52/3m, Looyen fell out of sight behind his comrades. He was then set upon by a patrol of Bf 109s of III./JG 26 and shot down east of Rotterdam; the kill was credited to Unteroffizier Matthias Massmann of 7./JG 26.

After refuelling and rearming at Ruigenhoek, Plesman and Roos were again dispatched to the area around Den Haag at 0900hrs. They did not encounter any enemy fighters but they did observe a number of Ju 52/3ms touching down on the beaches; these were transports carrying Luftlande troops which had been unable to land at their designated airfields. Plesman and Roos strafed several of the transports stuck in the sand near Katwijk and then flew on to Schiphol. Sitter, Bodaan, and de Geus took off from Schiphol for patrols before 1000hrs. They encountered a flight of three German bombers headed east but were unable to catch up to them. Despite the ferocity of the morning's combat and the overwhelming number of German aircraft in Dutch air space, seven of 2ᵉ JaVA's D.XXIs were back at Schiphol by late morning.

Ironically the Fokker T.V bombers of BomVA had more success against the German attackers in their first sorties than the fighters of 2ᵉ JaVA. The bombers warmed up their engines and taxied toward the runway as they waited for the fighters to take off. Then, one by one the bombers roared into the air amidst the falling bombs. The last T.V in line to take off, no. 859, had its hydraulic system damaged by bomb fragments while taxiing however and had to be abandoned. Initially BomVA was under orders to form three-aircraft patrols

A number of Ju 52/3ms were unable to land their cargo of Luftlande troops at the airfields around Den Haag and made emergency landings on the beaches to the west of the city, sinking into the soft sand. Several were attacked and set on fire by the fighters of 2ᵉ JaVA, operating from Ruigenhoek Airfield, after their initial battle over Schiphol on the morning of 10 May. (Courtesy of the Douglas Dildy Collection)

and to take up station over Aalsmeer, Buiksloot, and Haarlem, and await further orders; shortly after take-off however the squadron commander, Kapitein J.G. Sissingh, came on the radio and ordered his crews to immediately engage the attackers as best they could. BomVA's T.Vs were to serve in the luchtkruiser role for which they had been designed in a rare case of bomber-killer aircraft in combat during World War II.

As with the D.XXIs over Schiphol, there was no coordination among the aircraft of BomVA Three of the bombers, 850, 855, and 862 were to the south of Schiphol around 0440hrs when they observed a group of 11 German aircraft flying northwest at low altitude; these were Ju 52/3m transports of I./KGrzbV.172 carrying Fallschirmjäger for the paradrop over Valkenburg. T.V no. 862, commanded by 1ᶜ Luitenant Hans Metzlar, targeted one of the three-aircraft formations and attacked all three, scoring hits on each transport; one of the Ju 52/3ms went down and ditched in the sea south of Katwijk at 0450hrs. T.Vs no. 850, commanded by 1ᶜ Luitenant Peter Wildschut, and no. 855, led by 2ᶜ Luitenant Bernardus Swagerman, waded into the Ju 52/3ms, together shooting down one of the transports which crashed in flames near Leiden. After this combat, 850 touched down at Bergen to refuel and later returned to Schiphol while 862 landed at Ruigenhoek. 855 pursued the surviving Ju 52/3ms after they made their paradrops and near Utrecht damaged one of the transports so severely that it crashed upon landing.

T.V no. 865 had perhaps the most harrowing experience of BomVA's aircraft. After take-off its crew realized that the landing gear could not be retracted due damage to the hydraulic system. For some time, with its wheels down, it engaged German aircraft over Schiphol before suffering additional damage and making an emergency landing at De Kooy. The remaining bombers of T.V also battled the Germans but with no success; 853, 854, and 856 landed at Ruigenhoek while 858 touched down at Vlissingen. All of BomVA's aircrews survived their first wartime sortie.

Despite damage to the hangars and destruction of a number of aircraft parked in them, the attack on Schiphol was not a complete catastrophe for the Dutch. Fortuitously, the main runway was not damaged during the bombardment and Schiphol was once again made operational later that day once the bomb craters on the tarmac were filled in with rubble. To the east of the airfield, the munition magazine for the airfield's ground defences suffered a direct hit but the bomb failed to detonate, allowing the airfield's anti-aircraft batteries to remain operational. In the Fokker Company hangar, ten Fokker G.1B fighters, stored there awaiting delivery to export customers, were only lightly damaged and were easily repairable.

After the attack Fokker engineer and test pilot Frans Stok quickly took inventory of the G.1Bs: 342, 343, 346, and 347 had been test-flown and were partially armed while the remaining 350, 352, 356, 357, 360, and 361 were either untested or unarmed. Fearing the possibility of another German attack, Stok ordered the Fokker ground personnel to disperse the G.1Bs along the Haagweg

Fokker T.V 862 of BomVA, flying in the T.V's originally intended role as a luchtkruiser, shot down a Ju 52/3m of I./ KGrzbV.172 over Valkenburg on the morning of 10 May. (Courtesy of the Douglas Dildy Collection)

highway just outside the airfield. Branches from nearby trees were used to camouflage the aircraft and their aluminium propellers were painted black to prevent glare from the sun. Later on 10 May, trucks began delivering parts and weapons for the G.1 Wasps and Fokker mechanics set up an ersatz maintenance facility along the highway; efforts to make several of these aircraft combat-ready continued throughout the remainder of the campaign.

Attack on Bergen

About 20 miles to the north-west of Schiphol at Bergen airfield, the fighter pilots of 4ᵉ JaVA had been on alert since 0145hrs when word of the large neutrality violation reached the base. The squadron's 12 operational Fokker G.1A fighters were towed to the concrete tarmac adjacent to hangars 5 and 6 at the north-west corner of the base and arranged in three rows facing south towards the airfield. Mechanics warmed up the engines while 4e JaVA's commander, Kapitein Theodorus Lamers, phoned the C.-Lvd. in Den Haag at 0245hrs, requesting permission to send up a patrol of 2–3 aircraft to observe the large aircraft formation. The C.-Lvd. denied his request, stating that fighters could only be dispatched by order of the Jachtgroep commander or by squadron commanders after visual confirmation. At 0315hrs, the engines on the G.1As were switched off but their crews were told to remain on standby. The G.1A crews were not pleased that their aircraft were all parked in close proximity on the tarmac. Bergen did not have a paved runway however and during earlier dispersal exercises the heavy G.1A fighters sank into the moist grass during the early-morning hours; it took considerable time and effort to pull them out. The airfield was located near the sea, sitting just behind the sand dunes, resulting in damp conditions and there were some swampy sections on the field that heavier aircraft had to avoid. Given the unprecedented size of the foreign aircraft formations overhead that morning, Lamers wanted to make sure there was no delay in getting his fighters airborne if necessary. Also stationed at Bergen was the Strat.V.A. reconnaissance squadron with its ten operational Fokker C.Xs. Strat.V.A.'s biplanes were lighter than the G.1A fighters and were dispersed on the northern and southern sides of the airfield; a camouflage tent covered each aircraft. Strat.V.A. was not placed on alert and its aircraft crews, who were quartered in the village of Bergen, remained asleep in their bunks.

At 0359hrs, a red signal flare was spotted to the west, coming from the coastal lookout station at Egmond aan Zee; Lamers then received a phone call from the lookout station, informing him that three 'Blenheim' bombers had been spotted, coming in from the southwest at medium altitude and heading towards the airfield. Lamers immediately ordered his ground crews to start the fighters' engines. The 'Blenheims' were in fact the first of five Ju 88s of 7./KG 4 under the command of Hauptmann Erich Blödorn. 7./KG 4's mission had not started out well; Ju 88 5J+HR crashed and burst into flames shortly after take-off at Delmenhorst, leaving Blödorn's remaining five aircraft to carry on. One of the pilots in the remaining Ju 88s was Hans-Joachim 'Hajo' Herrmann, who became a successful bomber Gruppenkommandeur and later, as a night fighter Geschwader commander, was instrumental in the development of the Luftwaffe's night fighter *Wilde Sau* tactics. Both Blödorn and Herrmann were particularly eager to prove themselves on this mission. While on a landing approach at Fornebu Airport at Oslo earlier that April, Herrmann, piloting an He 111 of 7./KG 4 with Blödorn aboard as an observer, had embarrassingly overshot the runway and crashed, damaging his aircraft. As Blödorn's small unit turned towards Bergen as they approached the Dutch coast, they broke away from the group of 12 He 111s of KGr 126, which were also assigned to attack the airfield. The Ju 88s climbed to 3,000m while the He 111s maintained an altitude of 100m. Once over the airfield, Blödorn and Herrmann found to their delight the 12 Fokker G.1s of 4ᵉ JaVA parked close together. As Blödorn rolled over and commenced his dive-bomb attack, KGr 126's He 111s flew around the airfield from the south in order to make an attack run from the north. No Dutch fighters were observed in the air; surprise had been achieved at Bergen. The Ju 88s targeted the hangars, particularly Hangars 5 and 6 adjacent to the parked G.1s, while the He 111s attacked the remaining hangars and parked aircraft.

As the Ju 88s began their dives, Lamers ordered his pilots to scramble and engage the enemy. G.1A 321, piloted by 1ᵉ Luitenant Johan Thijssen, was in the top left corner of the parked formation and as its engines were already turned over, Thijssen taxied to the eastern side of the airfield and took off. Sergeant A.K. Bosman, in G.1A 331 which was second from the right in the front row of aircraft, had just begun to taxi when a German strafing attack hit his left engine, causing it to seize; the right engine, still running at increased power, caused the aircraft to suddenly turn to the left and nearly collided nose to nose with G.1A 304 of 1ᵉ Luitenant H. Dill. Lamers ran over to 331 to assist Bosman in moving his aircraft but took a bullet in his heel and the two officers headed for cover in a shelter trench. To the right of the bunched-up 331 and 304, a mechanic was busily trying to turn over the engines of the G.1A (either 322 or 325 but not known definitively) of 2ᵉ Luitenant Antoinne Van Ulsen but a strafing German aircraft caught the mechanic in its sights, killing him; no other mechanics were immediately available to start the aircraft. On the far left of the second row of fighters, the G.1A (either 322 or 325) of 1ᵉ Luitenant Otto Thate had its engines running but for reasons unknown Thate left the cockpit and did not immediately return; his gunner then switched off 304's engines and ran for cover. These incidents, all of which happened

Damage to Bergen Airfield, photographed after the Luftwaffe's early-morning raid. Fokker G.1As 313 and 317 of 4ᵉ JaVA were destroyed in Hangar 5 (right background), 331 and 333 were hit and burnt out on the tarmac (centre foreground and background), and 310 (left background) was damaged by bomb blasts. (Courtesy of the Douglas Dildy Collection)

Fokker G.1A 318 of 4ᵉ JaVA camouflaged and under repair on the Hoeverweg highway near Bergen Airfield later in the morning on 10 May. 4ᵉ JaVA ground crews are headed for cover as the air raid siren is being sounded. The Luftwaffe made several attacks against Bergen during the Meidagen. (Collectie Nederlands Instituut voor Militaire Historie)

within moments of each other, blocked the remaining G.1As in the second and third rows from taxiing away and as a result their crews took cover.

Without enemy fighter opposition, the German attack on Bergen proceeded largely unhindered. Blödorn's Ju 88s made direct hits on the base's hangars, including a direct hit on G.1A 333, located at the bottom right of the parked aircraft formation. The He 111s, dropping groups of smaller 50kg bombs, caused additional damage to the hangars, destroyed Bosman's 331, damaged other G.1As on the tarmac, and obliterated the base's motor pool. Three of KGr 126's He 111s sustained damage from anti-aircraft fire but the Luftwaffe lost no aircraft in its initial attack on Bergen. In addition to the damage listed above, two G.1s, 313 and 317, were undergoing maintenance inside Hangar 5 but were burnt out after catching fire from the bombs dropped on the hangar. Four aircraft belonging to Strat.V.A., Fokker C.Xs 704, 707, and 710 which were undergoing maintenance in Hangar 1 as well as a Fokker C.V utility aircraft, were destroyed when the hangars were hit as well. Amazingly, the ten operational C.Xs for Strat.V.A., which were dispersed around the airfield, were not spotted by the German attackers and suffered no damage. After the attack, Lamers assessed the damage; while the hangars were largely destroyed, maintenance equipment inside could be salvaged and a number of the G.1s on the tarmac had damage which could be repaired. Lamers had the six repairable G.1s, 308, 310, 318, 321, 322, and 325, towed south of the airfield and parked on the Hoeverweg highway, where camouflage netting and branches were placed over them. A mobile workshop was set up and repair work began almost immediately. In a stroke of good fortune, two soldiers saved one of the base's fuel trucks from destruction when they drove it out of a hangar to cover during the bombardment. Craters on the runway and tarmac were easily filled and the airfield was quickly made operational.

While the bombardment was taking place, Lt. Thijssen and his gunner, Sergeant K. Vermaat, in G.1A 321 attempted to engage the attacking bombers but found themselves the target of frantic anti-aircraft fire from the airfield's defenders. Thijssen veered to the northeast and came upon several of the attackers headed back for Germany. As Thijssen fired on the retreating bombers, he saw in the distance the ominous sight of 14 Bf 109s coming in from the north; he then wisely broke contact and headed to the south. As he passed over the smoke billowing from Schiphol, Thijssen spotted a lone He 111 and gave chase but his intended prey was able to evade the attack and dived away at high speed. As he climbed following this attack, Thijssen saw a T.V (856) in the distance over Haarlem;

several times he attempted to fly alongside and contact the bomber with hand signals but each time the G.1A approached, the bomber veered off, taking evasive action. By this time 321 was cruising above the coast and Thijssen observed seven Ju 52/3ms stranded on the beach near Katwijk. After making strafing runs on the hapless transports and setting three on fire, Thijssen headed for the airfield at Ypenburg to land. As he approached the airfield, the anti-aircraft batteries opened fire, the gunners mistaking the G.1A for a Bf 110, and Thijssen gunned the engines, making a hasty escape. Out of ammunition and nearly out of fuel, Thijssen decided to return to Bergen, narrowly evading a patrol of four Bf 109s, before finally touching down at 0620hrs. Thijssen taxied 321 to the Hoeverweg where it joined the other remaining G.1As for repairs. This turned out to be the only mission flown by the 4ᵉ JaVA on 10 May but the furious repair work by Bergen's ground crews ensured that the squadron would take part in future battles during the Meidagen.

Attack on De Kooy

Shortly before 0400hrs at De Kooy Airfield in the far north of Holland, Kapitein Schmidt Krans, commander of the 1ᵉ JaVA, heard the sound of multiple aircraft coming from the north. Like the other fighter squadrons, Schmidt Krans had received Best's alert message and the 11 Fokker D.XXIs of 1ᵉ JaVA were warmed up at 0300hrs and its pilots were on standby. Schmidt Krans called the Jachtgroep command in Den Haag, enquiring about the aerial activity to the north but was asked to hold by a staff officer; while he remained on the line, Schmidt Krans overheard another phone call in the background, and heard something about an attack on an airfield. Putting two and two together, Schmidt Krans dropped the phone and ordered his pilots to scramble. At 0359hrs, when the staff officer got back on the line, ordering Schmidt Krans to send up his fighters, all of 1ᵉ JaVA's aircraft were already airborne and forming their patrols.

Without orders and not immediately observing any aerial activity, the four patrols of 1ᵉ JaVA circled De Kooy for some time. Eventually the pilots observed smoke rising from De Vlijt and Bergen and individual patrols flew off to investigate. Luitenant Bram van der Stok in D.XXI 234 however, picked up a radio message that an He 111 had been spotted south of De Kooy and led his patrol away to intercept. Van der Stok and his wingmen, *Wachtmeester* (sergeant) W. Hateboer in D.XXI 244 and Wachtmeester Jaap van Zuylen in D.XXI 223, found the lone He 111 (likely from KGr 126) and briefly made an unsuccessful attack. Worrying that they were wandering too far from De Kooy, van der Stok signalled his wingmen to return but van Zuylen must not have received or understood the signals. Van Zuylen continued the pursuit of the He 111 to the south and later came across another pair of He 111s. At 0435hrs, 223 was observed, from the ground, being hit by the defensive fire of two He 111s and then crashing into the ground near Wassenaar; van Zuylen was presumably killed in the air by the He 111s' fire as 223 flew along for a while before crashing.

At 0420hrs, Hateboer, on his way back to De Kooy, spotted a Ju 88 and broke away from van der Stok to pursue. Hateboer easily manoeuvred behind Ju 88 5J+IT of 9./KG 4 and fired into it, sending it crashing down into the beach at Noordwijkerhout, to the southwest of Schiphol. Low on ammunition, Hateboer brought 244 in for a landing at Schiphol where it was rearmed and refuelled. Van der Stok was the only member of his patrol to return to De Kooy after this first sortie. Further to the south, 1ᵉ Luitenant F.L.M. Focquin de Grave in D.XXI 218 led his patrol to investigate the smoke rising over Bergen. He and his wingmen, 2ᵉ Luitenant H.J. van Overvest in D.XXI 219 and 2ᵉ Luitenant Jan Bosch in D.XXI 241, spotted a group of five Bf 109s over Bergen and pursued them for a while to the east but were unable to catch up with them. Neither of the other two patrols, led by 2ᵉ Luitenant Herman Doppenberg in D.XXI 221 and 1ᵉ Luitenant H.A.J. Huddleston Slater in D.XXI 214, engaged any enemy aircraft and shortly after 0430hrs they along with van der Stok landed at De Kooy to rearm and refuel.

At 0445hrs, after the other patrols had taken off again, Focquin de Grave led his patrol in to land, refuel and rearm. As Focquin de Grave made his landing approach, he saw ground personnel waving at him and running away from the landing area. He looked behind him and saw a group of Bf 109s coming in from the west; it was a group of nine Bf 109Es of II.(J)/Tr.Gr.186 which had been tasked with a strafing attack against De Kooy. Focquin de Grave gunned his engine and banked away from the airfield. Bosch, who was on approach behind Focquin de Grave, did not see the Bf 109s approaching behind him and as he touched down 241 was raked with machine-gun fire as several Bf 109s sped by overhead; 241 caught fire but Bosch was able to get out of the damaged aircraft. Van Overvest, who was on approach following Bosch, saw four Bf 109s behind him and immediately pulled up, performing an Immelmann over his pursuers. Bosch's 241 was to be the only success achieved in this sortie by the attacking Bf 109s of II.(J)/Tr.Gr.186; they were not expecting to encounter Dutch fighters over their target.

Huddleston Slater and his wingman, 2ᵉ Luitenant Jan Tuininga in D.XXI 240, as well as van der Stok were already at patrol altitude when the German fighters swept over the airfield and dived to attack the invaders. Focquin de Grave and van Overvest also immediately engaged the Bf 109s while Doppenberg and his wingmen, Sergeant G. Slag in D.XXI 233 and Sergeant Pieter Smits in D.XXI 242, joined the fight a few minutes later; they had to be recalled after they intercepted a Ju 52/3m to the south. For the next 15 minutes, the D.XXIs proved their superiority over the Bf 109s in a turning battle over De Kooy.

The Bf 109s attempted to form a large wheel over the airfield and then individually would make high-speed frontal attacks against the Dutch fighters. The German pilots were unable to hit the D.XXIs due to a combination of poor shooting and the superior manoeuvrability of the Dutch fighters and eventually, likely out of frustration, began to stalk their prey in turning fights.

Pilots of 1ᵉ JaVA at De Kooy Airfield; from left to right: 2ᵉ Luitenant H.J. van Overvest, 1ᵉ Luitenant F.L.M. Focquin de Grave, and 2ᵉ Luitenant Jan Bosch. Focquin de Grave and van Overvest each claimed a Bf 109 from II. (J)/Tr.Gr.186 in the battle over De Kooy. (Collectie Nederlands Instituut voor Militaire Historie)

2ᵉ Luitenant Jan Bosch (in the foreground, wearing a helmet) stands in front of the burning wreck of his Fokker D.XXI 241; the Dutch fighter was strafed while landing by raiding Bf 109s of II.(J)/Tr.Gr.186 after 1ᵉ JaVA's first sorties on 10 May. (Collectie Nederlands Instituut voor Militaire Historie)

Here the D.XXIs immediately got the upper hand, operating in twos with one fighter going after a German while the second held back to provide protective cover. Focquin de Grave managed to shoot up a Bf 109 (identity unknown), which broke away and limped off toward the east; it later made a forced landing on the German island of Borkum. Doppenberg got behind the Bf 109 piloted by Unteroffizier Wilhelm Rudolf and shot it down; Rudolf, badly injured, made a forced landing near the village of Anna Paulowna to the southeast of De Kooy.

Van der Stok was covering Doppenberg when the latter made his kill but shortly after, 234 came under fire from a Bf 109 making a head-on attack. Van der Stok dodged the attacker and turned to pursue. After three complete circles van der Stok got on the German's tail; the German pilot realized this and attempted to shake off his pursuer in a dive but inadvertently positioned himself right into 234's crosshairs. Van der Stok fired, hitting the Bf 109 (identity unknown) and sending it down in flames into the Ijsselmeer.

Shortly afterwards, van Overvest pulled up alongside van der Stok; 219 had been damaged but van Overvest signalled with a thumbs-up, meaning he too had achieved a kill. By this time the survivors of 5.(J)/Tr.Gr.186 were bugging out to the east and the remaining fighters of 1ᵉ JaVA began landing at De Kooy, clearly the victors of this battle. After landing van Overvest was able to inspect his kill, which had made a forced landing on the airfield; it was the Bf 109E-1 of Staffelkapitän Dieter Robitzsch. The German pilot, taken prisoner upon landing, was furious over the affair and impertinently asked the Dutch pilots, 'why do you resist?' Van Overvest and his colleagues were thoroughly amused with this encounter.

1ᵉ JaVA had achieved four kills without loss, but the remaining serviceable D.XXIs had all sustained damage and required repair. Around 0800hrs a small group of Bf 110s made a brief strafing attack on De Kooy that seriously damaged D.XXIs 214 and 233 and that injured Huddleston Slater; afterwards it was decided to cannibalize 214 and 233 in order to repair the remaining seven D.XXIs. II.(J)/Tr.Gr.186 was somewhat avenged when some of its fighters, alongside the Bf 110s of 2./ZG 76, caught the D.XXIs of 1ᵉ JaVA on the ground in another strafing attack around 1200hrs; D.XXI 234 was destroyed as well as T.V 865 which had landed at De Kooy after the raid on Schiphol. Despite the heavy fighting throughout the morning and the frequent raids, six D.XXIs were found to be salvageable and De Kooy's ground crews worked furiously throughout the rest of the day to make them operational.

Luftwaffe airborne operations within the Vesting Holland

Not long after Putzier's initial bombardment wave attacked the ML's airfields, the aircraft of the second bombardment wave began their flak-suppression missions. Beginning around 0450hrs, large formations of Ju 52/3ms began arriving over the drop zones for the Fallschirmjäger. The road and rail bridges at Moerdijk were captured intact with relative

The Bf 109E-1 of Staffelkapitän Dieter Robitzsch on De Kooy Airfield after being shot down by 2e Luitenant H.J. van Overvest in Fokker D. XXI 219. (Collectie Nederlands Instituut voor Militaire Historie)

ease by the two companies of II./FJR 1, transported by the 52 Ju 52/3ms of IV./KGzbV.1, which also secured the surrounding area by 1030hrs. One company of I./FJR 1was ambushed and shattered shortly after landing by Dutch garrison troops outside of Dordrecht but the remainder of the battalion, dropped by the 53 Ju 52/3ms of II./KGzbV.1, was able to capture the road and rail bridges over the Oude Maas. They maintained a tenuous hold on the bridges for the next several days, but their position was constantly threatened by the 1,500-man garrison in Dordrecht.

Shortly before 0500hrs, the 53 Ju 52/3ms of II./KGzbV.1 approached Waalhaven from the east and dropped the 700 paratroopers of III./FJR1 to the south and the east of the airfield. After consolidating, they assaulted the airfield. Despite putting up fierce resistance, the Dutch defenders were not prepared for an assault by such a large number of paratroopers; furthermore, gun emplacements and defensive hardpoints were positioned to cover the airfield itself and the Fallschirmjäger were able to take many of them from their exposed rear. Apart from the assault on the airfield, the 40-odd men of 11./FJR1 were dropped near the De Kuip football stadium in Feijenoord. After landing, these troopers commandeered a passing tram and several civilian autos and rushed to the southern end of the bridges spanning the Maas in the centre of Rotterdam.

Around 0510hrs, in what was perhaps the most outlandish of Student's operations that morning, 12 old Heinkel He 59 floatplanes of KGr.zbV.108 (Sonderstaffel Schwilden) touched down on the Maas in the middle of Rotterdam, six planes on each side of the bridges. After taxiing to the northern ends of the bridges, 120 infantry and *Pioniere* disembarked in small rubber boats and succeeded in capturing the northern bridgeheads. By around 0630hrs, Waalhaven airfield was in German hands and by the end of the morning, the route from Moerdijk to Rotterdam was secured; initial victory had been achieved in the southern theatre of Unternehmen F.

An He 59 floatplane of the Sonderstaffel Schwilden, observed by bewildered Dutch civilians, taxiing on the Nieuwe Maas towards the Willemsbrug traffic bridge in Rotterdam at 0510hrs on 10 May. (Collectie Nederlands Instituut voor Militaire Historie)

The airborne and airlanding operations in the northern theatre around Den Haag were a completely different matter however. Between 0445 and 0500hrs, Fallschirmjäger units were dropped around

KEY

 Airfield

 Airborne assault

EVENTS

Moerdijk

1 0400. 30 Ju 87s from IV.(St.)/ LG 1 conduct dive-bombing attacks against the antiaircraft batteries and infantry trenches on both sides of the road and rail bridges crossing the Hollandsch Diep as well as the Willemsdorp Barracks on the northern bridgeheads.

2 0450. 52 Ju 52s of IV./KGzbV.1 drop the two companies of II./FJR 1 on both sides of the bridges which, after consolidating, assault and capture the bridges intact.

3 1030. Fallschirmjäger secure the area around the bridges and set up a defensive perimeter.

4 1645. Fokker C.Vs 592, 605, and 622 of IIIe Verk. Gr. attack the Moerdijk southern bridgeheads. 622 is damaged and makes a forced landing.

Dordrecht

5 0450. 53 Ju 52s of II./KGzbV.1 drop the companies of I./FJR 1 around the road and rail bridges crossing the Oude Maas at Dordrecht.

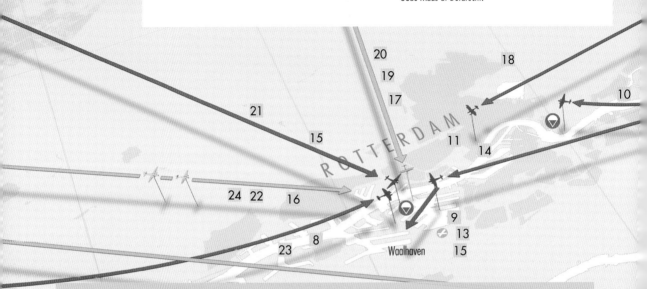

EVENTS

6 0630. One platoon from 3./FJR 1, having landed at Zwijndrecht, secures the northern bridgeheads and the bridges themselves. The remainder of 3./FJR 1, on the southeast edge of Dordrecht, are ambushed and put out of action by the instructors and students of the 1e Depotcompagnie Pontoniers en Torpedisten, stationed in the city.

7 0700–1600. The remaining companies of I./FJR 1 march from Tweede Tol and attack Dutch positions south of Dordrecht, eventually securing the southern bridgeheads by mid-afternoon. 1,500 Dutch troops remain in the city of Dordrecht and continue to fire on the German positions around the bridges.

Waalhaven Airfield/Rotterdam

8 0355–0445. 18 He 111Ps of II./KG 4 bomb Waalhaven.

9 0500. 53 Ju 52s of II./KGzbV.1 drop the 700 Fallschirmjäger of III./FJR1 to the south and the east of Waalhaven Airfield. 11./FJR1 is dropped near the De Kuip football stadium in Feijenoord. One Ju 52 is lost to flak on its return flight.

10 0510. 12 He 59s of KGr.zbV.108 land alongside the bridges crossing the Nieuwe Maas in Rotterdam and disembark 120 troops of 11./IR 16 and 2./Pi.22 which capture the bridges. 11./FJR1 secures the southern bridgeheads at 0600.

11 0555. Dutch Marines, stationed in Rotterdam, begin a push against the Germans north of the Nieuwe Maas and eventually contain them to the area directly around the northern bridgeheads.

12 0600. 53 x Ju 52s of III./KGzbV.1, carrying the 569 troops of III./IR 16, approach Waalhaven to land but the airfield's flak batteries have not yet been silenced. Four Ju 52s were shot down en route by G.1s of 3e JaVA while another three were shot down by flak on landing approach.

13 0630. III./FJR1 captures and secures the airfield and begins neutralizing nearby antiaircraft batteries. Undamaged transports are able to take off and return to Germany.

14 0800–1000. Torpedo gunboat Z-5 and torpedo boat TM-51 of the Koninklijke Marine sail up the Nieuwe Maas and attack German positions around the bridges. They also destroy four He 59s of KGr. zbV.108, still moored by the bridges. The warships are attacked by Ju 88s of II./KG 30 around 0935 but are not damaged.

15 0945. 22 x Ju 52s of IV./KGzbV 1, carrying two companies of I./IR 65, land at Waalhaven after diverting from Ockenburg and Ypenburg. At 0950 46 x Ju 52s of III./KGzbV 1, on their second sortie of the day, land at Waalhaven, delivering General Student, his staff, and two companies of II./FJR2. At 1000–1400 Ju 52s of II., III., and IV./KGzbV 1 deliver additional Luftlande troops, artillery pieces, and antiaircraft guns in staggered flights throughout the late morning and early afternoon.

16 1125. Six Blenheim IFs from No. 600 Squadron RAF attack Waalhaven but are intercepted by Bf 110s of 3./ZG 1; five Blenheims are shot down.

Luftwaffe operations around the southern front (Moerdijk – Rotterdam area) of Unternehmen F, 10 May 1940

EVENTS

17 1145. Fokker C.Xs 706, 708, 709, 711, and 712 of Strat.V.A. attack Ju 52s on the ground. On their return to Bergen they are intercepted by Bf 109s; 708 and 709 were both damaged and made forced landings.

18 1200. The two batteries of the I-10.RA artillery battalion, positioned north of the Nieuwe Maas in Rotterdam, begin a bombardment against Waalhaven Airfield. 675 shells are fired throughout the afternoon, destroying 11 Ju 52s.

19 1240. T.Vs 854, 856, and 862, escorted by D.XXIs 213, 224, 235, 236, 238, and 239, bomb the airfield, destroying three Ju 52s. Upon return, this group is intercepted by nine Bf 109s of 6./JG 27. D.XXI 238 and T.Vs 854 and 862 were shot down and D.XXI 239 was written off after landing. Four Bf 109s likely lost.

20 1245. Fokker C.Vs 606 and 614 of IVe Verk.Gr. attempt to attack Waalhaven but are intercepted by Bf 110s. 606 is shot down and 614 is strafed on the ground after an emergency landing. Credited

to Leutnant Egon Trotha of Stab III./JG 3 and Leutnant Leonhard Göttmann of 7./JG 3.

21 1430. Seven Ju 52s of 1./KGrzbV 9, carrying 14./IR 65 and four 7.5cm field guns, divert from Ockenburg and approach Waalhaven. One Ju 52 is lost to flak en route.

22 1440. Nine Blenheim IVs of No. 15 Squadron RAF bomb Waalhaven while the six transports of 1./KGrzbV 9 are offloading. One transport and two artillery pieces are destroyed.

23 1500. Attempting to repeat the earlier success of Z-5 and TM-51, the Koninklijke Marine sends the destroyer *Van Galen* up the Nieuwe Maas to bombard German positions around the bridges. The Germans call in Stukas from IV.(St.)/LG 1 which attack and heavily damage *Van Galen*; the destroyer sinks at its moorings later that day.

24 2050–0220. 36 Vickers Wellington bombers from No. 3 Group RAF, attacking in waves of nine aircraft, drop 60 tons of bombs on Waalhaven.

ML reconnaissance photo of Valkenburg Airfield taken mid-morning on 10 May. Note the numerous Ju 52s stranded on the airfield, stuck in the soft soil and the parachutes (white specks) of the Fallschirmjäger that landed in the vicinity. The battles for the airfields around Den Haag resulted in a disaster for the Luftwaffe. (Collectie Nederlands Instituut voor Militaire Historie)

Valkenburg, Ockenburg, and Ypenburg, but few of the paratroopers came down near their intended drop zones. Most were dispersed which meant that when they landed, much valuable time was wasted consolidating and then covering the distance to the airfields. The primary reason for this was that the crews of the Ju 52/3ms flying these missions were largely inexperienced in precision airborne operations. Kampfgeschwader zur besonderen Verwendung 2, whose squadrons were assigned to the northern theatre of operations, was hurriedly organized in the spring of 1940, specifically for Graf von Sponeck's Den Haag plan, and staffed with recent flight training graduates or Deutsche Lufthansa crews. This unit had received little specialized training and practice compared to the squadrons of Kampfgeschwader zur besonderen Verwendung 1.

It was intended that the Fallschirmjäger secure the landing area at each airfield prior to the arrival of incoming Luftlande units. However, due to their scattered dispersal, this was not achieved at any of the three airfields. The first wave of transports delivering Luftlande units at each airfield was met with varying degrees of ground fire which destroyed a number of transports upon final approach and after landing. These destroyed and damaged aircraft, littering the landing areas, subsequently hampered and even prevented further landings by incoming transports.

Circumstances at each airfield posed their own unique challenges to the attackers as well. Incomplete intelligence brought about a catastrophic failure at Valkenburg. The airfield was not yet fully operational and its landing area had not yet been reinforced for the use of heavy aircraft. Every Ju 52/3m that landed there sank up to its belly in the soft soil, still damp in the early-morning hours. Not a single Ju 52/3m that landed at Valkenburg that morning was able to take off again. Faulty intelligence resulted in disaster at Ockenburg as well. The headquarters of the Koninklijke Leger's elite Regiment Grenadiers was located in the nearby village of Loosduinen; shortly after capturing the airfield and Ockenburg, the Fallschirmjäger and Luftlande troops there came under coordinated Dutch counterattacks.

At Ypenburg, the flak suppression bombardment carried out by I./KG 30 failed to effectively neutralize the anti-aircraft batteries around the airfield. As a result, the first two waves of Luftlande transports were subjected to a murderous fire upon landing approach; 19 Ju 52/3ms of these two waves were lost upon landing while the surviving Ju 52/3ms diverted and either landed where they could or returned to Germany. The Fallschirmjäger and Luftlande troops that eventually converged on the airfield could not fully secure it as they were unable to dislodge the defenders from the northern end of the field. The soft soil at Valkenburg and the ground combat at Ockenburg and Ypenburg precluded any further landings at the airfields by mid-morning; the only reinforcements the embattled troops on the ground received were from Ju 52/3ms that made forced landings in nearby fields and beaches or that landed on highways.

By noon, Kesselring and his staff realized that the operations around Den Haag had completely fall apart. Only around 3,500 troops had been deployed, roughly 35 per cent of the intended total, and they had been landed in no less than 14 different locations. Reinforcements could not be deployed to the landing areas because of a lack of transports; too many had been lost in the early delivery missions. In the early afternoon, units of the Ie Legerkorps, the strategic reserve of the Koninklijke Leger stationed within the Vesting Holland, had already begun the process of closing in on and recapturing the three airfields.

By late afternoon, the airfields were back in Dutch hands, with over 1,000 prisoners taken, and the surviving Fallschirmjäger and Luftlande troops were driven into the dunes and woods west of Den Haag; around 1,000, including Graf von Sponeck, remained at large until the end of the campaign. Before the end of the first day of the Meidagen, the northern theatre of operations of Unternehmen F had become irrelevant to the course of the Luftwaffe's campaign in the Netherlands. Pockets of Germans received occasional supply drops over the next several days but tactical support could not be had due to limited communication and increasingly limited numbers of aircraft. By 14 May, 2,735 of Graf von Sponeck's troops had been killed, wounded, or sent to Great Britain as prisoners of war.

Back at Waalhaven, Ju 52/3ms of II./KGzbV.1, III./KGzbV.1, and KGR.zbV.172 began ferrying in Luftlande reinforcements throughout the remainder of the morning and early afternoon. Some reinforcements included Luftlande units originally destined for the airfields around Den Haag, but their transport pilots, part of IV./KGzbV.1, diverted to Waalhaven after observing the chaos on the ground. These early operations were not without losses however; in addition to four Ju 52/3ms of III./KGzbV.1 shot down by the G.1s of 3ᵉ JaVA, 12 Ju 52/3ms were lost to anti-aircraft fire and another two to landing accidents in flights into Waalhaven before 1100hrs.

A little before 1000hrs, General Student landed at Waalhaven with his staff and was, overall, pleased with 7.Fliegerdivision's successes at Moerdijk, Dordrecht, and Rotterdam. This optimistic outlook began to drastically change a little over an hour later. Around 1145hrs, five Fokker C.X biplanes approached from the west at an altitude of 2,500m. Flying level, they dropped small-calibre bombs over the southern end of the airfield which damaged a number of the transports parked there. The Dutch attackers were C.Xs 706, 708, 709, 711, and 712 from StratVerVA, whose aircraft escaped destruction during the earlier raid on Bergen. Shortly after bombing Waalhaven, the C.Xs were intercepted by eight Bf 109s of 6./JG 27; C.Xs 708 and 709 were forced down but the remaining three returned to Bergen. While this was only a minor raid, it was a portent of things to come for the Germans at Waalhaven; the striking power of the ML and the Dutch will to resist had not been broken.

The wreck of Fokker C.X 709 of StratVerVA, forced down after a bombardment mission against the Ju 52/3ms at Waalhaven shortly before noon on 10 May. (Courtesy of the Douglas Dildy Collection)

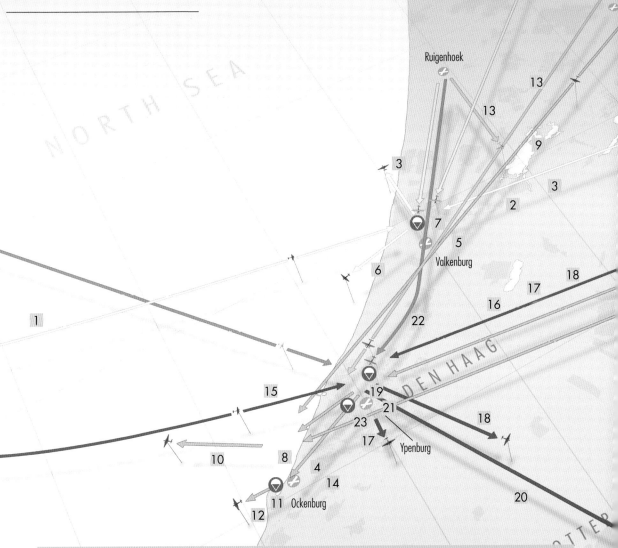

KEY

 Airfield

 Airborne assault

EVENTS

Landeplatz I – Valkenburg Airfield

1 0415hrs. A Kette of He 111s from II./KG 4 bomb and strafe Valkenburg's hangars.

2 At 0445hrs, six Ju 52s of 4./KGrzbV 172 overfly the drop zones around Valkenburg and drop two platoons from 6./FJR2 on the beaches around the airfield.

3 At 0520hrs, 53 Ju 52s of KGrzbV 11, carrying the regimental staff IR 47 and the III./IR 47 infantry battalion, approach Valkenburg to land. 50 land but sink into the soft soil, unable to take off again. One is shot down on approach and two others divert to nearby beaches at Katwijk. At 0600 Fallschirmjäger and Luftlande troops secure the airfield.

4 At 0610hrs, seven Ju 52s of KGrzbV 12, diverted from Ypenburg, land at Ockenburg and sink into the ground. With 57 transports stuck on the airfield, further landings are impossible.

5 0830hrs. The Dutch III-2.RA artillery battalion takes up position near Valkenburg and begins a bombardment of the airfield for the rest of the morning which destroys over a dozen Ju 52s. At 0830 Fokker C.Vs 605, 619, 621, 622, and 631 of IIIᵉ Verk.Gr. attack the Ju 52s stuck in the ground.

Luftwaffe operations around the northern front (Den Haag area) of Unternehmen F, 10 May 1940

EVENTS

6 At 0905hrs, 39 Ju 52s of 2., 3., and 4./KGzbV.1 approach Valkenburg but abort landing after seeing the congestion on the airfield. Three are shot down by anti-aircraft fire on their approach, 20 head back to Werl, and 16 land along the beaches to the west.

7 At 1120hrs, Fokker C.Xs 713, 714, and 715 of StratVA drop 21 50kg bombs over the Ju 52s, destroying six. Between 1600hrs and 1730hrs, 4ᵉ Regiment Infanterie assaults and retakes the airfield, capturing around 100 Germans and forcing the surviving 500–600 Fallschirmjäger and Luftlande troops to retreat into the village of Valkenburg. By this time only 16 of the 57 Ju 52s stuck in the soil on the airfield are undamaged.

Landeplatz II – Ockenburg Airfield

8 0430–0445hrs. D.XXIs 217 and 228 of 1-V-2 and DB-8As 389 and 391 of 3-V-2 land to rearm and refuel at Ockenburg after the débâcle over Ypenburg. There is no fuel on the base and the aircraft are grounded.

9 At 0445hrs Bf 110s of II./ZG 1 strafe the airfield.

10 0455hrs. Most of the 13 Ju 52s of 16./KGzbV 1 overfly the drop zones around the airfield and widely disperse the Fallschirmjäger of 3./FJR 2, with some paratroopers landing in the North Sea and drowning. One Ju 52 is shot down by flak before reaching Ockenburg.

11 At 0524hrs, 18 Ju 52s of 3./KGrzbV 12, carrying troops of the staff IR 65 and 5./IR 65 infantry regiment, land at Ockenburg. The Luftlande troops engage the airfield garrison and combat engulfs the airfield, destroying and damaging a number of the transports. At 0605hrs, 15 Ju 52s of 1./KGrzbV 9 approach Ockenburg, carrying bicycle reconnaissance troops of 2./N. Abt. 22 signal company. Eight land at Ockenburg, three land to the southwest, three abort landing at Ockenburg due to ground fire and make forced landings on the beaches near Kijkduin, and one is shot down by flak after diverting. No other aircraft are able to land at Ockenburg; only four are able to take off and return to Germany. At 0700hrs, Luftlande troops secure the airfield.

12 0705hrs. Ten Ju 52s of KGrzbV 9, having diverted from Ypenburg, land on nearby beaches and fields after observing the combat at Ockenburg. Ju-52 9P+BL of 3/KGr zbV 9, carrying General Graf von Sponeck, lands between Ockenburg and Ockenrode.

13 0715–0730hrs. Fokker T.V 855, flying from Schiphol, and T.Vs 854, 856, and 862, flying from Ruigenhoek, attack the airfield with 50kg and 100kg bombs, destroying six Ju 52s. T.V 855 is shot down over the North Sea off Kijkduin by Oberleutnant Victor Mölders of 1./ZG 1.

14 0800. The Dutch I-2.RA artillery battalion begins a bombardment of the airfield, destroying another 12 Ju 52s. At 1100–1430, supported by artillery, the first battalion of the *Regiment Grenadiers*

begins its assault to take back the airfield. Graf von Sponeck and around 350 Luftlande troops retreat to the woods west of Ockenburg; almost 200 are taken prisoner at the airfield. At 1430 Ockenburg is back in Dutch hands. 22 destroyed or damaged Ju 52s are left on the airfield.

Landeplatz III – Ypenburg Airfield

15 0400–0445. He 111s of 1./KG 4, and Bf 110s of II./ZG 1 attack Ypenburg. Ju 88s of I./KG 30 conduct a flak suppression mission but fail to destroy the airfield's anti-aircraft defences.

16 0445. 40 Ju 52s of IV./KGzbV 1 approach Ypenburg and drop the Fallschirmjäger of 1./FJR2. One Ju 52 is shot down by flak en route to Ypenburg, four are shot down on the return flight, and two crash upon landing. 1./FJR2 is widely dispersed and unable to consolidate and capture the airfield prior to the arrival of incoming Luftlande transports.

17 0524. 36 Ju 52s of KGrzbV 12, carrying elements of the IR 65 infantry regiment, come into Ypenburg for a landing but are fired upon by the airfield's anti-aircraft batteries and ground defences. 13 Ju 52s are destroyed upon landing and the remainder divert, landing where they can.

18 0605. 40 Ju 52s of KGrzbV 9, carrying the staff of the 22. Luftlande-Division as well as reconnaissance troops and Pionere, attempt to land. Six were destroyed upon landing and the others divert, with a number landing on the highway between Delft and Rotterdam.

19 0715. Fallschirmjäger and Luftlande troops capture most of the airfield but are unable to neutralize Dutch defensive positions at the northern end of the airfield which continue to fire upon incoming aircraft.

20 0906. 26 Ju 52s of IV./KGzbV.1, carrying more troops of IR 65, approach Ypenburg. One Ju 52 is shot down by flak en route while most divert to Waalhaven. All remaining scheduled transport flights to Ypenburg are cancelled or diverted to Waalhaven.

21 1100. The second battalion of the Regiment Grenadiers, supported by the guns of the II-2.RA artillery battalion begin a counter-assault to retake the airfield.

22 1250. Fokker C.Vs 631, 639, and 645 of the III.Verk.Gr. attack Ypenburg with 25kg bombs.

22 1510. Nine Bristol Blenheim IV bombers of No. 40 Squadron RAF attack Ypenburg.

23 1530. The Dutch retake the airfield and almost 1,300 Fallschirmjäger and Luftlande troops are taken prisoner. 17 Ju 52s destroyed on the airfield and many others destroyed or damaged after diverting elsewhere.

Militaire Luchtvaart counterattacks

By 0630hrs in Den Haag, the Commando Luchtverdediging was already beginning to recover from the initial shock of the Luftwaffe's airfield attacks as well as the Fallschirmjäger assaults on the airfields and bridges. It quickly launched the first of a series of retaliatory attacks against German positions inside of the Vesting Holland. At 0700hrs, T.Vs 854, 856, and 862, which had landed at Ruigenhoek after the air battle over Schiphol, were dispatched to attack the Ju 52/3ms on the ground at Ockenburg; T.V 855, which had returned to Schiphol, was also sent on this raid. On approach, the Dutch bomber pilots counted 27 transports on the field at Ockenburg and once over the target the T.Vs dropped their 50kg and 100kg bombs, destroying six Ju 52/3ms. T.Vs 854, 856, and 862 then headed west toward the coast and dropped to an altitude of 25m to avoid being spotted and safely returned to Ruigenhoek. T.V 855, which was flying on its own, was not as fortunate. Shortly after attacking Ockenburg, it was intercepted by Bf 110s of 1./ZG 1 and shot down over the North Sea off Kijkduin by Oberleutnant Victor Mölders. Only the aircraft's commander, Lt. Swagerman, survived and swam ashore. By this time of the morning, it was clear that all of the ML's frontline squadrons had been engaged and had sustained heavy losses. The only squadrons which had escaped the Luftwaffe's onslaught relatively unharmed were StratVerVA at Bergen and the Verkenningsgroepen. With no other aircraft available, the C.-Lvd. launched several raids with its old C.V and C.X biplanes against the airfields around Den Haag and the transports landing on the motorways and beaches nearby. By late morning the C.-Lvd. ascertained that the German-held airfields around Den Haag could no longer receive reinforcements and decided to concentrate its remaining strength against Waalhaven, where German reinforcements were being flown in. The attack made by the C.Xs of StratVerVA was the result of this decision.

Generaal Best had also formally requested assistance from the British Royal Air Force through the British deputy air attaché in Den Haag, recommending that the British bomb Waalhaven as soon as possible and render it unusable. The C.-Lvd.'s request for a bombardment of Waalhaven was initially held off by the British government, which was concerned about diplomatic fallout if Dutch civilians were killed in such a raid. Initially, it recommended that only fighters be allowed to attack Waalhaven in a precision strike. At 1125hrs, six Bristol Blenheim IF heavy fighters from No. 600 Squadron RAF swept over Waalhaven and strafed several Ju 52/3ms on the ground. They caused little damage as they were quickly intercepted by patrolling Bf 110s of 3./ZG 1, which shot down five of the attackers. Given this disaster and continuing Dutch requests for bombing raids, the British government authorized Bomber Command to attack Waalhaven and other targets in the Netherlands at the request of the Dutch. Before the day was over, RAF Bomber Command launched small raids against Waalhaven, Ypenburg, and the Ju 52/3ms stuck on the beaches west of Den Haag. Dutch requests for further assistance, particularly fighter support, had to be ignored due to the Luftwaffe's simultaneous onslaught against airfields in Belgium and Northern France.

Shortly after the first British attack upon Waalhaven, the ML struck the airfield again. After their raid on Ockenburg, T.Vs 854, 856, and 862 were recalled to Schiphol to rearm for

Fokker T.V 854 of BomVA made a successful attack against the Ju 52/3ms at Ockenburg Airfield on the morning of 10 May but was shot down early that afternoon in an attack against Waalhaven Airfield. (Courtesy of the Aviation Museum Aviodrome, Netherlands)

Fokker C.V 605 was one of three aircraft of IIIᵉ Verk.Gr. which made an afternoon attack against German troops dug in around the bridges at Moerdijk. (Courtesy of the Douglas Dildy Collection)

a bombing raid on Waalhaven; this time however, the C.-Lvd. decided to wait until a fighter escort was available for protection. By late morning, ground crews at Schiphol had managed to make six D.XXIs of 2ᵉ JaVA combat ready and at noon these fighters were ordered to escort the three T.Vs to Waalhaven. At 1215hrs this force took off, led by Lt. Bodaan in D.XXI 238, with Sgt. Burger in 213, Sgt. de Geus in 224, Lt. Plesman in 235, Lt. Sitter in 236, and Sgt. Carel Steensma (a KLM pilot who volunteered that morning for active duty with 2ᵉ JaVA) in 239. Once airborne this attack force assembled into three V-formations and flew at an altitude of 500m, just below light cloud cover. Several times the formation leapt above the clouds to avoid roving German fighters. On approaching Waalhaven, 20–30 transports were counted on the airfield and the T.Vs concentrated their attack against the eastern end of the field where most were parked. While the T.Vs made their bombing run, Sitter dived and made a strafing run against several transports while his colleagues remained overhead.

There was little time to examine the damage done however for when Sitter pulled up, he saw the escort being set upon by Bf 109s from 7./JG 3 and I./JG 26. Most of the German fighters went after the D.XXIs and a swirling dogfight took place over the airfield in which Plesman, de Geus, and Steensma each made hits on the attackers. Bodaan was not so fortunate on this mission however. Unteroffizier Herbert Springer of 7./JG 3 got behind D.XXI 238 and riddled it with bullets, sending it crashing down near Rhoon, south of Waalhaven; Bodaan was killed. Unfortunately, the D.XXIs were not able to prevent several of the Bf 109s from going after the T.Vs and 854 and 862 were both shot down; they were credited to the Staffelkapitän of 3./JG 26 Oberleutnant Johannes Seifert, who went on to become an ace with 57 kills, and Feldwebel Ernst Biegert of 2./JG 26.

Sitter observed the attack on the T.Vs and went after the German fighters, which had not observed his strafing run. Sitter got behind one of the attackers and got into a turning fight in which he eventually prevailed, sending the Bf 109 down; the identity of Sitter's opponent is still unknown. T.V 856 managed to evade the German fighters and made it back to Schiphol. D.XXIs 213, 224, 235, 236, and 239 limped back as well, all landing by 1310hrs. Steensma's 239 was so badly damaged however that it had to be written off. It had been a costly mission for the ML, four losses sustained to one inflicted, but it had surprised the Germans, particularly the number of ML aircraft involved.

After the raid against Waalhaven, the ML's fighters remained out of combat for the rest of the day. Although losses to personnel had been relatively light, losses to aircraft had been very heavy. 17 D.XXIs and 17 G.1As had been destroyed or written off. At 1400hrs, the C.-Lvd. decided to concentrate its remaining single-engine fighters into a single Combined JaVA and ordered the surviving D.XXIs of 1ᵉ JaVA, 2ᵉ JaVA, and 1-V-2 to assemble at Buiksloot Airfield, just north of Amsterdam.

Buiksloot opened in 1938 as a civil gliding airfield but was taken over as an auxiliary airfield by the ML after the start of the war. It had not been targeted by the Luftwaffe during the initial attacks because German intelligence was not aware of its military use. While the airfield's terrain was rather poor and soft, the C.-Lvd. reasoned that the lack of enemy attention made it a safe place to operate from. Around 1600hrs, D.XXIs 212, 213, 224, 225, 235, and 236 flew from Schiphol to Buiksloot, and they were joined there later that evening by 218 and 244 from De Kooy. Only one G.1A, 303 which was undamaged in the Fokker hangar at Schiphol, was operational after the morning's combat and was also sent to Buiksloot.

Ground crews at Bergen worked throughout the remainder of the day to repair several of 4ᵉ JaVAs G.1As while Fokker, KLM, and ML mechanics worked to make several of the G.1Bs, housed at Schiphol, operational. BomVA had only two remaining operational T.Vs, 850 and 856, and these were kept at Schiphol; the remaining 12 T.Vs had been lost or written off. Thus, only a handful of frontline combat aircraft were operational by the end of 10 May but a number of second-line aircraft remained operational: the eight surviving C.Xs of the StratVerVA as well as the surviving C.Vs the Verkenningsgroepen.

The ML's midday attack on Waalhaven was not the last attack made against the German-held airfield on that day. C.Vs 606 and 614 of IVᵉ Verk.Gr. struck the airfield almost immediately after the T.Vs made their bombing run. Both were lost to the patrolling Bf 109s. Nine Blenheim IVs of No. 15 Squadron RAF struck unopposed at 1440hrs and damaged a number of transports. More worrying to Student than these raids however was that, beginning at around noon, Waalhaven had come under artillery bombardment. Throughout the morning, Dutch ground forces had consolidated their defences around the northern bridgeheads in Rotterdam and the I-10.RA artillery battalion had positioned its two batteries on the northern edge of the Nieuwe Maas. The Dutch guns rained 675 shells down on the airfield for the remainder of the afternoon. By late afternoon the damage from the aircraft and artillery bombardments had rendered the airfield largely unusable. 36 Ju 52/3ms had been destroyed by the bombardments. By the end of the day, Student's transports had made 210 sorties into Waalhaven and there were roughly 3,700 Fallschirmjäger and Luftlande troops tenuously holding a narrow corridor from Moerdijk to Waalhaven. Dutch ground forces had rallied throughout the day however and had limited the German forces to this corridor. There could be no further gains on the ground unless reinforcements could be landed or until the Panzers of 18.Armee

ML reconnaissance photo of Waalhaven Airfield taken at 1500hrs on 13 May. The buildings and hangars were destroyed during the Luftwaffe's early-morning raid on 10 May but most of the other craters are from the ML's and RAF's raids of the airfield as well as the Koninklijke Leger's artillery bombardment. It is evident why the airfield was of only very limited use to Student's forces throughout the Meidagen. (Courtesy of the Douglas Dildy Collection)

arrived. The onset of darkness did not bring any peace for Student either. Between 2050 and 0220hrs, 36 Wellington Mk.I bombers, each carrying 18× 100kg bombs, from No. 3 Group RAF attacked Waalhaven in groups of nine aircraft. Each group carried out individual bombardments, staggered at ten-minute intervals in an effort to erode the morale of the Germans on the ground. By 0300hrs, another 13 transports had been destroyed on the ground and substantial damage had been caused to the landing area, enough to prohibit any further large-scale landing operations. For the time being, Student and his airborne troops were on their own, deep in enemy territory.

Operations from 11 to 14 May 1940

Throughout the night of 10–11 May, the staff of Luftflotte 2 were in a near panic at General Kesselring's headquarters in Münster. The operations of Gruppe Nord around Den Haag had been a complete disaster. That evening Kesselring had the unpleasant task of sheepishly informing Göring of the failure of the Den Haag operation. Recognizing that any further attempts to reinforce or support Gruppe Nord would be futile, he instructed Graf von Sponeck to attempt to make his way towards Rotterdam and join up with Student's forces. He also had to report that Student's successes in the Moerdijk-Rotterdam area were qualified at best. The gateway into the Vesting Holland was open, but just barely. With Dutch ground forces closing in all around the Moerdijk-Rotterdam corridor, Student was in desperate need of reinforcements. Since Waalhaven's landing field had been rendered largely unusable during the earlier afternoon and evening, getting reinforcements into the area would be difficult at best.

It was clear what had to be done; Waalhaven and the Moerdijk-Rotterdam corridor had to be defended at all costs if any success was to be salvaged from Unternehmen F. This meant keeping Student's forces supplied, attempting to reinforce them, and giving them tactical ground support when possible. Supply and reinforcement would be a challenge to say the least; there were plenty of Luftlande troops available for deployment but few transports available to deliver them. Only some of the roughly 140 transports of KGzbV.1 and KGzbV.2 that made it back to Germany on the 10th were available as many had been damaged and needed repair. Tactical support was primarily limited to the remaining bombers of Putzier's Fliegerkorps zbV.2 and several fighter units of Döring's JaFu 2. Putzier was also required to support the drive of the 18.Armee in the southern Netherlands as the bulk of Luftflotte 2 was committed to supporting the advance of 6.Armee through Belgium, as well as keeping pressure on British and French squadrons in the region. The 18.Armee would need support too; reconnaissance flights discovered that French motorized units, the spearhead of a larger armoured force, were moving northwards into the Netherlands, heading for Moerdijk. For the remainder of the Meidagen campaign, the objective for the remaining Luftflotte 2 units assigned to Unternehmen F became keeping the Moerdijk-Rotterdam corridor open long enough for 18.Armee to arrive. The final problem Luftflotte 2's staff had to account for that evening was the strikes made against German positions in the Vesting Holland throughout 10 May by ML aircraft; Dutch air power had not been completely neutralized and still had to be contended with.

The evening of 10–11 May, was also restless for the Commando Luchtverdediging and the morning of 11 May revealed a sobering reality. The heavy aircraft losses sustained on the previous day meant that the ML's ability to provide air defence for the Vesting Holland had been effectively eliminated; air defence had to be left to surviving anti-aircraft batteries. It was acknowledged that the Luftwaffe had gained air superiority over the Vesting Holland and that this would remain the case until Allied fighter squadrons could intervene. This would not be anytime soon as the RAF had turned down Dutch requests to base British fighter squadrons at Dutch airfields. While the ML had taken a beating on the first day of the invasion, the

Ju 52/3m of KGzbV.1, camouflaged with tree branches, after making a forced landing near Moerdijk due to damage sustained by Dutch anti-aircraft fire on 11 May. After the heavy damage sustained at Waalhaven from aerial and artillery bombardments on 10 May, Student's forces were reinforced primarily by Ju 52/3ms landing and taking off along the highway between Moerdijk and Dordrecht. (Collectie Nederlands Instituut voor Militaire Historie)

Koninklijke Leger had held the German 18.Armee along the Grebbelinie in the central part of the country and its units in southern Holland were pressuring the Moerdijk-Rotterdam corridor held by Student's airborne troops. The 18.Armee had breached the northern end of the Peel-Raamstelling and on the morning of 11 May, Dutch army units abandoned this line for an improvised defensive line to the west.

The German plans to drive through the southern Netherlands to the corridor into the Vesting Holland were clearly apparent to the Dutch and Allied leadership. The French promised to send armoured units northward and assist the Dutch with a defensive stand near Breda; these units would also assist the Koninklijke Leger in the recapture of the bridges at Moerdijk, closing the door into the Vesting Holland to the oncoming Panzers. Generaal Best wisely concluded that the most judicious use of his remaining aircraft was to bolster the army's efforts in holding its defensive lines until French reinforcements arrived and assisting the army in containing Student's airborne forces. The ML was down but it was not out; it could still deliver limited tactical support but its pilots would have to employ evasive measures, flying at low altitudes, to avoid the seemingly ever-present German fighter umbrella over the theatre. For the remainder of the Meidagen campaign, the ML committed itself to what was essentially a guerrilla campaign against the Luftwaffe and German ground forces.

The morning of 11 May began with Luftflotte 2's staff concluding that only the timely arrival of 18.Armee's Panzers at the Moerdijk-Waalhaven corridor held by Student's troopers could save Unternehmen F. Most of the morning and early afternoon was spent examining reconnaissance reports of what was actually happening on the ground in the Netherlands and bolstering Student's forces. The situation was initially judged to be so dire that, at 0400hrs without consulting Student, the staff of Luftflotte 2 dispatched a Fallschirmjäger reserve company to be dropped by parachute near Dordrecht. Of the 12 Ju 52/3ms of IV. IV./KGzbV.1 that transported Kompanie Moll, three were shot down by Dutch anti-aircraft fire upon approach to the drop zone. The Fallschirmjäger that did land at Kop van't Land, southeast of Dordrecht, were contained by Dutch troops from the city garrison and unable to join Student's forces. This impulsive action demonstrated the limited knowledge which Kesselring and his staff had at the time and their desperation to salvage the campaign.

Later that morning, Student did begin to receive reinforcements when a section of the highway between Moerdijk and Dordrecht was cleared for use as an ersatz runway and transports from KGzbV.1 began delivering Luftlande troops. A small landing area was also repaired at Waalhaven but was only large enough to allow one transport to land, unload, and take off at a time; it was also subject to ongoing artillery fire from Dutch batteries north of the Nieuwe Maas, which further limited its use. Student's troops were once again receiving fresh troops and supplies, albeit at a trickle. He 111s of I./KG 4 were tasked with supply missions, dropping canisters to Fallschirmjäger and Luftlande troops under Student's command but also to pockets of Graf von Sponeck's scattered forces which were identified from the air.

Perhaps the most important action by Luftflotte 2 in supporting Student's beleaguered forces occurred on the afternoon of 11 May. The Dutch 6ᵉ Grense-Bataljon near Moerdijk was planning an attack against the German positions at the bridges in conjunction with lead elements of the French 25ᵉ Division d'Infanterie Motorisée, which had arrived in Breda the previous evening; armoured units of the 7ᵉ Armée were to follow later. Luftwaffe reconnaissance flights had observed the French movements, as had the Fallschirmjäger at Moerdijk who nervously requested air support. After confirmation of the impending French threat, General Putzier ordered the He 111s and Ju 88s of III./KG 4 to attack the villages around Moerdijk where French armoured cars and motorized infantry were assembling. Just as the French armoured cars were about to begin their attack around 1700hrs, the first of several waves of Luftwaffe bombers arrived on the scene and attacked. The Stukas of IV./LG 1 were likely employed as well and after nearly two hours of aerial attacks, with no fighter cover to protect them, the surviving French motorized forces retreated. Due in large part to the Luftwaffe's control of the skies over the southern Netherlands, the French withdrew from Breda on the 12 May and the promised French armoured support for the Koninklijke Leger was diverted elsewhere. This would leave the eastern approach to Moerdijk wide open for the advancing 9.Panzer-Division.

For the next several days, JaFu 2's fighters continued to be deployed on combat air patrol and Freie Jagd missions, although their patrol area was pushed further to the south and west as they also had to cover the 6.Armee's advance through Belgium. As a result of the continued Dutch air strikes throughout 10 May and over the remaining days of the campaign, JaFu 2 allowed its units to seek out Dutch aircraft on the ground and destroy them. On 11 May, the airfields at Texel, De Kooy, and Bergen were attacked by 2./ZG 76 and II.(J)/Tr.Gr.186. The aircraft at advanced training school at Haamstede were also attacked by II./ZG 1. Fighter pilots from these units claimed a large number of aircraft destroyed on the ground in these raids but they were only training aircraft with no practical combat value. During the remaining days of the campaign, Luftwaffe reconnaissance flights failed to observe the ML's aircraft on the ground at Ruigenhoek and Buiksloot or the resumption of flights from Schiphol and Bergen, spotting only training aircraft or damaged/dummy aircraft purposely left out in the open by ML ground crews. Luftflotte 2 staff assumed that the ML's ongoing operations were most likely originating from those airfields where Dutch aircraft had been spotted. As a result, Haamstede was attacked again on 12 and 13 May and Vlissingen was targeted on 13 and 14 May.

A Ju 87 Stuka of IV./LG 1 flying over Fallschirmjäger around Moerdijk. IV./LG 1's Stukas and the He 111s and Ju 88s of III./KG 4 were instrumental in halting the advance of French motorized forces towards Moerdijk on May 11. (Author's collection)

However, JaFu 2's ongoing limited fighter umbrella was never able to completely stifle Dutch aerial activity during the remaining days of the campaign. Döring's continuing fighter patrols did however allow Putzier's bombers to freely operate over the battlefront and ground-attack missions were flown in support of German operations along the Grebbelinie and in the Moerdijk-Waalhaven corridor. Operations were limited by the damage sustained by Putzier's bombers on the first day of the campaign and the need for He 111s of KG 4 to be used for supply drops to the airborne forces behind enemy lines. The Ju 87s of IV./LG 1 flew a number of precision strike missions against Dutch positions on the northern side of the Nieuwe Maas in Rotterdam but these seemed to have had little effect on the ground combat there. The Stukas had more success in hampering Dutch operations around the Moerdijk-Dordrecht areas as well as supporting the eventual drive of the 9.Panzer-Division onto the Island of Dordrecht on 13 May.

In Den Haag on the morning of the 11th, the staff of the Commando Luchtverdediging was also carefully weighing its options. With very little offensive capability remaining, the operations which the remaining aircraft of the ML could undertake were limited. One valuable service it could still provide for the army was reconnaissance flights, primarily with its C.V observation aircraft. There were just enough remaining D.XXI fighters to provide escorts for some of these flights as well. The ML had enough surviving aircraft to conduct reconnaissance flights for the remainder of the Meidagen campaign. At 0800hrs, the Combined JaVA at Buiksloot received reinforcements from De Kooy; D.XXIs 221, 240, and 242 had been repaired during the night and were flown over, bringing the number of available D.XXIs up to 11. The C.-Lvd. also decided to rearm its operational Fokker D.XVII biplane fighters, being used as advanced trainers at De Vlijt, and they were dispatched to Buiksloot that afternoon to reinforce the Combined JaVA.

It was not long before the limited strike capabilities of the ML were called upon, in this instance by the garrison commander of Rotterdam, Kolonel Pieter Wilhelmus Scharoo. Dutch ground forces attempting to eliminate the Germans' northern bridgeheads in Rotterdam had been under heavy machine-gun fire from German positions on Noordereiland on the southern bank of the Nieuwe Maas in central Rotterdam. This had also prevented artillery units from positioning batteries along the northern bank. Early that morning Scharoo decided that the destruction of the road and rail bridges provided the most prudent defence for the northern part of the city as well as the Vesting Holland and requested a bombing attack against the bridges from Generaal Best. As the importance of this mission was deemed

Fokker D.XVII 202 at the Jachtvliegschool at De Vlijt Airfield prior to the Meidagen. The old D.XVII fighters, then being used as advanced fighter trainers, were pressed into frontline service by the Commando Luchtverdediging on 11 May. (Courtesy of the Douglas Dildy Collection)

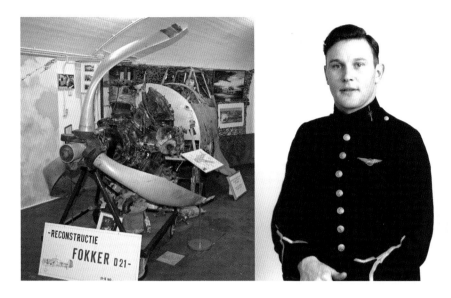

The only surviving remnant of the Fokker fighters that defended Dutch skies during the Meidagen is the engine and cockpit of Fokker D.XXI 229, discovered in 1993. 229, piloted by Sergeant Jacobus 'Koos' Roos (right), which was shot down by Bf 110s of 1./ZG 1 during the ML's second failed attack against the bridges in Rotterdam on 11 May. The remains of 229 are on display in the Stichting Crash 40–45 Museum near Schiphol. (D.XXI 229 – Author's collection; Roos – Collectie Nederlands Instituut voor Militaire Historie)

critical, the two remaining T.Vs of BomVA, with an escort of three D.XXIs, were tasked by the C.-Lvd. At 1010hrs, 1ᵉ Luitenant Franciscus Bik, in D.XXI 213, led Sgt. de Geus and Lt. Sitter, in D.XXIs 224 and 236, into the air. Four minutes later they rendezvoused with T.Vs 850 and 856 over Schiphol and headed south for Rotterdam. Incredibly, this small force arrived undetected over the city roughly 15 minutes later and there were no enemy fighters overhead. The two T.Vs executed a low-level bombing run against the bridges but their bombardiers released their bombs early; the 50kg bombs splashed down in the Nieuwe Maas, just short of their target. The bombers safely returned to Schiphol and the fighters to Buiksloot, both groups arriving at around 1045hrs.

After learning of the failure of the attack against the bridges over the Nieuwe Maas, the C.-Lvd. ordered another attack be made against them. Around 1300hrs, the T.Vs again took off from Schiphol and flew to Buiksloot, where they met their escort of three D.XXIs at 1309hrs: 1ᵉ Lt. Focquin de Grave in 213, Sgt. Roos in 229, and Sgt. Burger in 242. The attack force again arrived over Rotterdam undetected and the T.Vs began their bombing run at 1324hrs. This time the bombers lined up parallel with the bridges and approached them in a shallow dive from 1,200m. At 700m each bomber dropped eight 50kg bombs but the result was the same as before with the bombs landing harmlessly in the Nieuwe Maas. Unfortunately for the Dutch attackers, they did not get away unscathed this time. On their return flight they were intercepted west of Gouda by 12 Bf 110s of 1./ZG 1. Focquin de Grave turned and fired on the incoming German fighters, then dived away hoping to draw a number of the attackers away from the slower T.Vs. He succeeded as six of the Germans followed him. The other six Bf 110s split in half, with three going after Roos and the others targeting the T.Vs. After its rear gunner put up a spirited fight and two of their members were killed, the remaining crew of T.V 850 bailed out of their crippled bomber over Waddinxveen, just west of Gouda. 850 was credited to Oberleutnant Mölders of 1./ZG 1. While T.V 850 was under attack, T.V 856 banked into low cloud to lose the Germans. Its pilot then dived to the deck and skimmed his way back to Schiphol at an altitude of 10m.

Overhead, Focquin de Grave engaged in a turning dogfight for some time, damaging at least two of the Bf 110s. Eventually hit in the stomach by enemy fire, he disengaged and dived. He brought 213 down for a landing on the Den Haag-Rotterdam highway outside of Zevenhuizen but the aircraft overturned after striking the rail along a viaduct. Focquin de Grave managed to climb out of the cockpit and hid under the viaduct while the Bf 110s strafed the wreck of 213; he was later taken to hospital in Gouda.

OPPOSITE ML *HUISJES–BOOMPJES–BEESTJES*, OR HU·BO·BE, TACTICS

After the loss of two out of the five Fokker C.X biplanes of StratVerVA which attacked Waalhaven at 1145hrs on 10 May 1940, the pilots who returned to Bergen decided that a change in tactics was necessary if they were to have any chance of success in subsequent missions due to the Luftwaffe's overwhelming air superiority. The ML's pre-war tactics for ground strike missions called for attacks to be made from 2,500m. The slow speeds of the Fokker C.V and C.X biplanes conducting these missions made them sitting ducks for German fighters at that altitude, especially as, by this point in the campaign, Dutch fighters were already unavailable in sufficient numbers.

StratVerVA's pilots decided to adopt a low-altitude attack strategy in which they would approach their targets and return to base at as low an altitude as possible, using the dark green camouflage of their aircraft to hide themselves against the largely pastoral landscape of the Dutch countryside. When nearing their targets, they would have to quickly climb to an altitude of at least 300m as Dutch bombs had a safety device which would not allow them to detonate when dropped below that altitude. Furthermore, observers would have to aim their bombs by eye as the bombsights in their aircraft could not be calibrated to an altitude lower than 700m. It was a risky strategy as there would be little reaction time for pilots if attacked by German fighters when flying so close to the deck but the pilots of StratVerVA and the Verkenningsgroepen embraced it wholeheartedly. This low-altitude ground strike tactic became known as *Huisjes–Boompjes–Beestjes* (houses, trees, animals – as pilots dodged and skimmed over these), or HU-BO-BE. It was used with considerable success by C.V and C.X pilots for the remainder of the campaign, much to the consternation of German ground troops on the receiving end and to the frustration of Luftwaffe fighter commanders who could not ascertain where these attacks were coming from and how they were happening at all in light of their ever-present fighter umbrella.

Roos in 229 also put up a determined fight, perhaps more so than he initially intended. After taking damage from the Bf 110s, Roos decided to bail out and detached the canopy; to his astonishment, the canopy flew back and struck one of the engines of the Bf 110 on his tail. As this damaged attacker dropped away, Roos turned into some nearby clouds and, upon exiting, found himself on the tail of another Bf 110. Unfortunately, just as he was about to open fire on the unsuspecting German, 229 was hit by the remaining Bf 110, or possibly mistakenly by Dutch ground fire. This time, Roos was forced to bail out, badly wounded. He was taken to hospital in Leiden. Only Burger in 242 made it back to Buiksloot. Credited with one of the D.XXIs was Leutnant Wolfgang Schenk of 1./ZG 1, who earned another 17 kills during the war and went on to later become inspector of jet fighters for the Luftwaffe.

German aerial transport activity around Waalhaven was the primary concern of the Commando Luchtverdediging during the morning and early afternoon of 12 May. Reconnaissance had shown that further Luftlande reinforcements were being flowing into Waalhaven and other intelligence suggested that Student's troopers were preparing the car park of the Feijenoord Stadium to serve as a makeshift landing strip, although this latter report was later found to be false. At 1005hrs, the C.-Lvd. ordered StratVerVA to prepare for a raid on both the stadium parking lot and Waalhaven Airfield. At 1407hrs, the Combined JaVA was ordered to provide escort for the StratVerVA mission. Six C.Xs were detailed to this mission but ground crews at Bergen were unable to turn over the engines of C.Xs 714 and 715. Shortly after 1600hrs, C.Xs 705, 711, 712, and 713 took off from Bergen and arrived over Buiksloot at 1616hrs to rendezvous with their escort– D.XXIs 219 (Sgt. Slag), 221 (Lt. van der Stok), 224 (Lt. Bik), 235 (Lt. Plesman), and 244 (Lt. Bosch), led by Lt. Sluyter in D.XXI 212.

Unlike the attacks against the Rotterdam bridges the previous day, the attack force flew at a very low altitude, skimming over the ground and buildings at times. This low-altitude approach and departure tactic became known as *Huisjes-Boompjes-Beestjes* (houses, trees, animals – as pilots skimmed over these), or HU-BO-BE. It was implemented by C.V and C.X pilots, who were unescorted by fighters on their first missions, toward the end of the first day of the campaign as a means to offset the German advantage of air superiority. By flying on the deck, they could approach a target with a low chance of detection and, upon

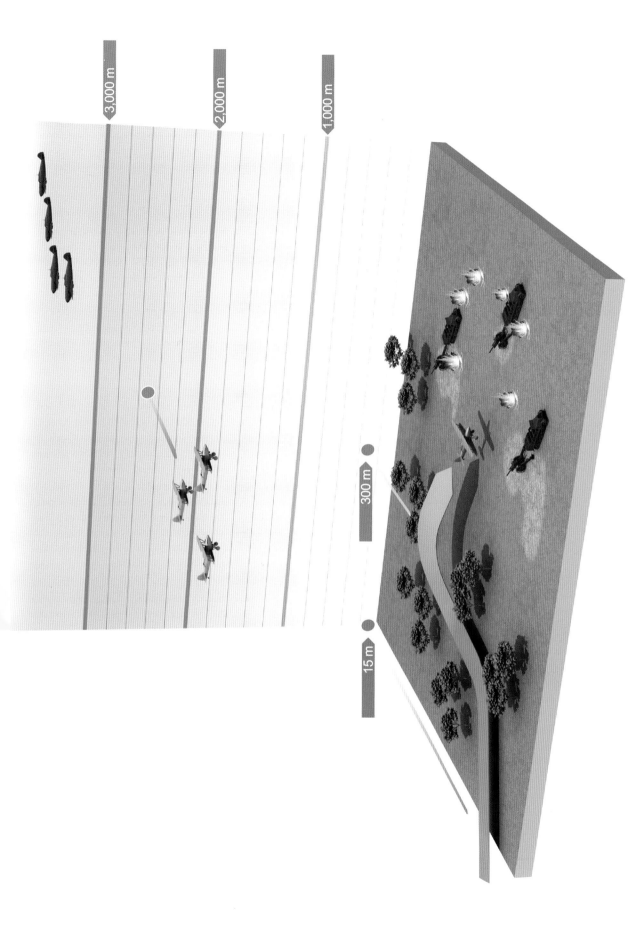

3,000 m

2,000 m

1,000 m

300 m

15 m

departure, it was difficult for the enemy to observe the attackers, even older biplanes, when they were close to the ground. On its approach to Rotterdam, the attack force divided up into two groups. C.Xs 712 and 713, covered by three D.XXIs climbed to 300m above the Feijenoord Stadium and bombed and strafed the parking lot and Luftlande troops gathered there. C.Xs 705 and 711, covered by the remaining D.XXIs, climbed to 350m and planted most of their bombs across the area of the landing field which the Germans had made operational. Both groups then dropped back down to the deck and made their way back to their airfields. HU-BO-BE had proved successful as a group attack tactic.

Beginning at 1240hrs that afternoon, a major German assault upon the Grebbelinie, spearheaded by the SS-Brigade *Der Führer*, broke through the frontal defensive line. During the course of the afternoon, the German advance threatened to breach the full depth of the line. Generaal Jan J.G., Baron van Voorst tot Voorst Jr., the commander of the Veldleger, phoned Generaal Best mid-afternoon and requested air strikes against the advancing Germans. After the German assault began, the C.-Lvd. ordered IIIe Verk.Gr. to make a reconnaissance flight over the Grebbelinie and assigned four D.XVIIs of the Combined JaVA to provide fighter escort. Three of the four D.XVIIs took off from Buiksloot at 1400hrs and flew to Ruigenhoek where they were to then take off with the C.Vs of IIIe Verk.Gr. Upon landing, the pilot of D.XVII 203 braked too hard and flipped his aircraft, 207 was heavily damaged after running off the landing field and 205 landed short of the airfield, striking the fence bordering the base; the pilots of the D.XVIIs were still trainees from the Jachtvliegschool who still had little advance flying experience. Without an escort, this reconnaissance flight was cancelled and ground crews went to work repairing D.XVII 205, the only salvageable fighter from the flight.

Over the next two hours, the situation became so desperate along the Grebbelinie that at 1600hrs, Opperbevelhebber van Land- en Zeemacht Winkelman personally phoned Generaal Best, immediately requesting all available air support the ML could provide. With the Combined JaVA and StratVerVA engaged over Waalhaven, Best phoned the 4^e JaVA at Schiphol where three G.1As were available. At 1615hrs, G.1As 303 (Lt. van Oorschot), 322 (Sgt. Henk Hartkoren), and 325 (Lt. Leegstra) scrambled and headed east; their orders were, in an effort to stabilize Dutch morale on the ground, to strafe German troops near Wageningen, advancing towards Rhenen on the Nederrijn. No German fighters were encountered on the way to or over the target so the G.1 pilots took their time strafing enemy

The old Fokker C.V biplanes of the Verkenningsgroepen were used extensively for reconnaissance missions and HU-BO-BE low-altitude attack missions throughout the Meidagen. Fokker C.V 634 of the ML survived both the Meidagen and World War II, and is housed in the Aviation Museum Aviodrome in Lelystad, the Netherlands. (Author's collection)

troop columns and positions. All of the G.1s sustained hits from mobile German anti-aircraft guns and the damage suffered compelled the pilots to land at Soesterberg Airfield, which was closer, around 1645hrs.

After Best dispatched the G.1s of 4ᵉ JaVA to the Grebbelinie, the 1ᵉ Verk.Gr. was also ordered to strike the German columns near Wageningen with all of its available aircraft. The only available escorts were D.XVIIs 210, piloted by Luitenant Johannes Stuy, 209, piloted by Jan Plesman (younger brother of 2ᵉ JaVA pilot Hans Plesman), and 205, piloted by Benjamin Moerkoert, which had been repaired at Ruigenhoek and had joined its colleagues at Middenmeer. At 1700hrs, C.Vs 594, 612, 646, 650, and C.X 719 took off with their three escorts and headed towards the Grebbelinie. Flying towards Wageningen at 150–200m, this attack force also escaped the attention of enemy fighters and then climbed to an attack altitude of 1,000m once near the target. In their attack dive, C.Vs 594 and 612 dropped their 50kg bombs into enemy troop positions. 612 was hit by German anti-aircraft fire during its initial attack run and then, mistakenly, by Dutch ground fire as it left the combat area. Its pilot was forced to make an emergency landing behind Dutch lines. C.X 719, which was not equipped with bomb racks, made several strafing runs against German troop columns. The observers of C.Vs 646 and 650 became confused during the attack and did not drop their bombs, fearful that they might mistakenly hit their own troops on the ground. All of the attackers, except C.V 612, were able to depart the combat area and all landed at Soesterberg around 1900hrs.

HU-BO-BE low-level ground strike by Fokker C.Xs, 0430hrs 13 May 1940

Prior to the Koninklijke Leger's planned counterattack against the German breach in the Grebbelinie on the morning of May 13, StratVA was called upon to make a ground strike against German artillery positions along the Grebbelinie at precisely 0430hrs. Generaal Best was determined to provide the maximum amount of cover for his few remaining strike aircraft and called upon the Combined JaVA and 4ᵉ JaVA to dispatch as many fighters as they could muster. At 0347hrs, Fokker C.Xs 700, 705, 711, and 712 took off from Bergen and headed towards Buiksloot to rendezvous with their escort. They were joined there by Fokker D.XXIs 235 (Lt. Plesman), 240 (Lt. van der Stok), 242 (Sgt. Smits), and 244 (Lt. Bosch), commanded by Lt. Doppenberg in 219. Fokker G.1As 318 (Lt. Frans Peetoom) and 321 (Lt. van Ulsen) from the 4ᵉ JaVA, also assigned as escort for this mission, departed Bergen at 0400hrs and met up with the rest of the force east of Buiksloot. Once assembled, the attack force dropped to an altitude of 50m and proceeded towards the Grebbelinie.

Just west of Wageningen, the C.Xs climbed to 350m, with the fighters climbing slightly above them to provide cover. Almost exactly at 0430hrs, the C.Xs dropped their 32 50kg bombs across the German artillery positions, damaging several guns and starting fires in the dense woods in which the artillery was camouflaged. With no enemy fighters in the vicinity, the escorting D.XXIs and G.1As began a number of strafing attacks against German positions and they were later joined by the C.Xs. After expending most of their ammunition, the Dutch aircraft departed the scene and headed back west at low altitude, employing HU-BO-BE evasive tactics. As there was cloud cover, along the route back to Bergen, Lt. van Ulsen climbed into the clouds. Coming out of a cloud bank over Woerden, he happened to find himself behind a flight of three Bf 109s from 1./JG 26. Van Ulsen gave the Bf 109 in the centre a heavy burst from his guns and then ducked back into the clouds before he could be pursued. All of the attackers returned safely to Buiksloot and Bergen shortly after 0500hrs. At 0725hrs Generaal Baron van Voorst tot Voorst Jr. pleaded with Generaal Best for another ground strike. Despite the exhaustion of his crews and equipment, Best obliged and requested volunteers for a second mission.

After a few hours of repairs, four C.Xs and five D.XXIs were again ready for combat; their targets were German columns moving along the roads between Wageningen and Rhenen. C.Xs 705, 711, 712, and 713 took off from Ruigenhoek at 1122hrs and again picked up their escort over Buiksloot. This time it was D.XXIs 224 (Lt. Bik), 236 (Lt. Sitter), 240 (Sgt. A. Postma), and 242 (Sgt. de Geus), commanded by Lt. van de Vaart in 212. As with the early morning's attack, no enemy fighters were encountered, another 32 50kg bombs were dropped on German positions, and despite heavy ground fire, the C.Xs and D.XXIs made several strafing runs against the Germans on the ground; all aircraft again returned safely. Almost all of the aircraft on these two missions received damage of some sort from enemy anti-aircraft fire.

Wreck of Fokker C.V 619 of IIIᵉ Verk.Gr. after it was forced down by a Bf 109E of Stab II./JG 27 behind the German lines along the Grebbelinie in the early evening of 12 May. Sergeant Antoon van Liempd (right) climbed out of the wreck and surrendered to a group of SS soldiers, who promptly executed the Dutchman. (C.V 619 - Courtesy of the Douglas Dildy Collection; Liempd – Collectie Nederlands Instituut voor Militaire Historie)

After the aircraft of 1ᵉ Verk.Gr. were called up for duty, a similar strike from IIIᵉ Verk. Gr. was ordered. IIIᵉ Verk.Gr.'s available C.Vs were returning from an aborted strike mission over Friesland when the call from Opperbevelhebber van Land- en Zeemacht Winkelman came in and, given that his crews had been active all day, upon landing the squadron's commander asked for volunteers for this next strike mission. Despite being told that no fighter escort would be available, his pilots' response was practically unanimous. Three C.Vs were able to be quickly rearmed and refuelled and three volunteer crews were selected. At 1832hrs, C.Vs 592, 605, and 619 took off to strike the German positions around Wageningen. Using HU-BO-BE tactics, the three biplanes approached the target undetected and then climbed to 800m to make their attack. This time, however, the Dutch attackers were met by German fighters over the target– the Bf 109s of Stab II./JG 27. Immediately, the C.Vs broke away and, making evasive manoeuvres, dived to the deck in an effort to escape. C.V 605 just cleared the ground as its faster pursuer shot by overhead. Hugging the deck the entire way, its pilot safely guided the aircraft back to Ruigenhoek.

As 592 was pulling up out of its dive away from the Bf 109s, its left underwing struck something on the ground and was torn away. Its pilot, Luitenant A.J. Eenkhoorn, pulled up trying to clear a dike in front of him but just caught the top of it, sending the aircraft flipping over into the ground. Amazingly, Lt. Eenkhoorn and his observer were able to walk away from this crash and were surprised to discover they had landed right in front of a Dutch defensive position; nearby medics attended to them immediately.

The crew of 619 was not so fortunate however. The aircraft was shot down by Hauptmann Walter Andres of Stab II./JG 27 and its pilot, Luitenant Theo Vrins, made a forced landing behind German lines. Vrins' observer, Sergeant Antoon van Liempd climbed out of the wreck and made his way over to a group of German soldiers with his hands in the air. Van Liempd was promptly shot dead by the Germans. Vrins, who remained hidden, witnessed this scene and stayed in hiding until later taken prisoner by a German patrol. It was apparent that the ML's air strikes had had an effect upon German morale. It is hard to measure the tangible effect of the ML's attacks on German troops around the Grebbelinie that afternoon. During the evening, Dutch ground forces began to stabilize the front somewhat, continuing to hold most of the rear area lines of the Grebbelinie.

Throughout the evening of 12–13 May, Generaal Baron van Voorst tot Voorst Jr. crafted a plan for a counterattack the next morning, designed to recapture the lost forward defences of the Grebbelinie. He again requested assistance from the C.-Lvd., hoping for ground strikes to silence some of the enemy's artillery batteries prior to sending his infantry over the top. Best phoned the commander of the StratVerVA at 0015hrs on 13 May, ordering a precision strike against German artillery positions near Wageningen at dawn. This strike was carried out at 0430hrs on 13 May, with fighter cover provided by D.XXIs and G.1As from the Combined and 4ᵉ JaVAs. A second similar strike took place shortly before noon *(for more details on these missions, see Battlescene 03)*. Despite the success of these missions, the Koninklijke Leger's counterattack slowed and then was blunted by a German counterattack. Throughout the early afternoon, Dutch ground forces were pushed back but, by mid-afternoon, had slowed and then stopped the German advance. The writing was on the wall for Baron van Voorst tot Voorst Jr. however. The German pressure against the Grebbelinie could not be relieved and, at 1700hrs, he initiated a full retreat from the Grebbelinie before it was completely breached. During the evening of 13–14 May, Dutch ground forces quietly withdrew west to the defences of the Waterlinie. When the Germans resumed their attack around 2100hrs that night, they were surprised to find the Dutch lines empty. Before any effective pursuit could be organized, the Dutch had slipped away.

The C.-Lvd. originally planned to use BomVA's last remaining T.V in the dawn attack at the Grebbelinie, in conjunction with the C.Xs of StratVerVA. By 0010hrs that morning, BomVA had been ordered to prepare T.V 856 for this mission, but at 0340hrs was ordered to stand down by the C.-Lvd., re-arm the bomber with two 300kg bombs, and report once this had been completed. With this completed by 0505hrs, BomVA was given its new mission – it was to attack and destroy the road bridge across the Hollands Diep at Moerdijk. During the late afternoon of 12 May, forward elements of the 9.Panzer-Division began to arrive at Moerdijk, after General Putzier's bombers had helped to clear their way of any French resistance the day before. It was not until the early morning hours of 13 May that Opperbevelhebber van Land- en Zeemacht Winkelman's staff were finally convinced that German panzers were preparing to breach the Vesting Holland. Dutch artillery was being moved into position on the Island of Dordrecht to shell the Moerdijk bridges but the ML was called upon to assist as well. As the T.V bomber was the only aircraft in the ML's inventory capable of carrying bombs of a calibre large enough to damage the bridge, T.V 856 was assigned to this mission and the aircraft would be commanded by the indomitable Lt. Swagerman – the only survivor of the crew of T.V 855 shot down after attacking Ockenburg on the morning of 10 May. Escort would be provided by G.1As 308 and 315 of the 4ᵉ JaVA,

Fokker T.V 856, photographed prior to mobilization, the last operational T.V of BomVA during the Meidagen, and its commander 2ᵉ Luitenant Bernardus Swagerman. Swagerman survived being shot down in T.V 855 and bailing out into the North Sea on the morning of 10 May, but lost his life when 856 was shot down after a failed attack on the bridges at Moerdijk on the morning of 13 May. (Courtesy of the Douglas Dildy Collection)

flown by 2ᵉ Luitenant Bodo Sandberg and 2ᵉ Luitenant Paul Schoute. A third G.1A from Bergen, 310 flown by Sgt. Bosman, was to be part of the escort as well. However, on the flight from Bergen to Schiphol, Bosman was unable to lower one of the landing gears and was forced to bail out, with the loss of 310.

At 0519hrs, T.V 856 and its two escorts took off from Schiphol and flew towards Moerdijk at low altitude. Upon reaching Dordrecht, 856 climbed to 1,000m and the G.1s took up positions 300m above the bomber on both sides. Swagerman and his crew were unable to attack the bridge from a lower altitude as a safety mechanism in the 300kg bombs dictated that they had to be released from an altitude of at least 300m in order to detonate. On the first bombing run, the bomb landed in the water roughly 50m from the bridge and exploded. On the next run, the bomb landed alongside one of the bridge pillars but, in a stroke of bad luck, failed to explode.

After this failed attack, the three planes dived away to make their return to Schiphol but as they passed over Dordrecht, they were intercepted by eight Bf 109s. The German fighters split up, pursuing each Dutch aircraft. Both T.V 856 and G.1A 315 were shot down in quick succession with no survivors. Only Sandberg, who briefly engaged several Bf 109s, was able to escape after diving to the deck and making a low-altitude getaway. With all of its T.Vs out of action, there could be no further attempts to destroy the bridges at Moerdijk by the ML. The back door to the Vesting Holland was now wedged open.

Superficially, the end of 13 May should have been a time of celebration for the Germans. The Dutch had abandoned the Grebbelinie and the first panzers of the 9.Panzer-Division had arrived at Waalhaven, much to the joy of Student and his hard-pressed Fallschirmjäger and Luftlande troops. Beneath the surface, however, there was exhaustion, frustration, anger, and recrimination.

Firstly, 18.Armee's commander, General von Küchler, was under increasing pressure from his superior, General von Bock to conclude his campaign in the Netherlands. The campaign was now in its fourth day (the day by which the Netherlands was supposed to have been subdued according to Fall Gelb's original timetable) and the Dutch still held the last barrier into the Vesting Holland, the Nieuwe Maas at Rotterdam. The journey of von Küchler's panzers from Moerdijk to Waalhaven had been far from swift or straightforward. In fierce street-by-street fighting, Dutch ground forces in Dordrecht had defeated 9.Panzer-Division's attempt to capture the city and the German panzers withdrew, bypassing the city on their way to Waalhaven and leaving at least 15 destroyed tanks behind.

General Bock, in turn, was being pressured by OKH to deploy the 9.Panzer-Division to the south where it could support the promising armoured advance in northern France that followed the decisive German victory at Sedan. Von Küchler and von Bock had both underestimated the ability of the Dutch to mount a fierce and effective defence that was inmpacting on Fall Gelb's carefully prepared and remorseless timetable.

That afternoon, von Küchler formed a new ground force – combining Student's airborne units, the 9.Panzer-Division, and the SS *Leibstandarte Adolf Hitler* –in preparation for the assault on Rotterdam the following day, placing it under the command of Generalmajor Rudolf Schmidt of the XXXIX.Armeekorps. At 1715hrs, von Küchler instructed Schmidt that all means available were to be used to end the Dutch resistance in Rotterdam. He also told Schmidt that it was his intention to breach the Rotterdam defences the following day and push on to Den Haag and Amsterdam with his armoured units while his forces at the Grebbelinie would push forward, threatening Utrecht and the Waterlinie. The capitulation of the Dutch government should quickly follow.

The situation at Luftflotte 2's headquarters on the evening of 13 May was even more heated than that at von Küchler's. While Putzier's bombers had decisively prevented French reinforcements from interfering with the 9.Panzer-Division's advance towards Moerdijk on 11 May, Student's forces had only held on by a thread at Waalhaven, supported by a perilously thin lifeline of transport flights into the beleaguered airfield. Most of Graf von Sponeck's remaining forces, including the General himself, were unable to reach Student's troopers, and had dug in near the village of Overshie, northwest of Rotterdam. In the skies over the Netherlands, despite air superiority, the Luftwaffe had proved unable to effectively support ground operations along the Grebbelinie or in Rotterdam. Perhaps the biggest embarrassment of all for Luftflotte 2, however, were the continuing ground attacks and aerial operations undertaken by the ML. While these operations caused only minor material damage and did little to significantly hinder German ground operations, they had impacted on the morale of German ground forces. To elements of the German high command, however, the ML's continued harassment and its role in undermining the success of Unternehmen F was a flagrant insult to the indomitable image of the Luftwaffe. With the exception of Student's operations, the Luftwaffe had, to all appearances, failed in almost every other aspect of Unternehmen F.

Hitler's precise reaction to the disaster at Den Haag – the operation he himself had been most enthusiastic about – has not survived but knowing his characteristic reaction to defeats and disasters, it is probable that choice words were used. We do know that he was outraged at the result. Göring, who probably bore the initial brunt of Hitler's anger, was also incensed at this blow to the prestige of the Luftwaffe – particularly its vaunted airborne arm. The consequences of the catastrophic losses suffered by his transport squadrons were just becoming apparent to him as well. He in turn ordered Kesselring to deal with the situation swiftly and decisively, instructing him that all means necessary were to be used to force the capitulation of Rotterdam, if not the entire Netherlands.

In Waalhaven that evening, Schmidt and Student worked out the details for their assault across the Nieuwe Maas the next morning. They both agreed that an aerial bombardment of Dutch defensive positions along the northern banks of the Nieuwe Maas was necessary, prior to an attack by Student's Fallschirmjäger and Schmidt's SS assault troops. Student conferred with Putzier, requesting a precision strike against known Dutch strong points around the bridges. He suggested the use of the Ju 87s from IV./LG 1 then requested from Kesselring the temporary use of the Ju 87s of I./StG 77 and II./StG 77 from the VIII.Fliegerkorps for this one mission. Student's justification for the use of the Stuka squadrons was that the dive-bombers were the only units capable of providing the precision strikes he needed. The bridges could not be damaged by the aerial bombardment and both

Tank of the 9.Panzer-Division stopped on a road in the Netherlands. Only the timely arrival of the 9.Panzer-Division at Moerdijk on the morning of 13 May spared Student's forces operating out of Waalhaven the same disaster that befell the airborne units around Den Haag. (Getty Images)

OPPOSITE AERIAL BOMBARDMENT OF ROTTERDAM BY KAMPFGESCHWADER 4, 1325HRS ON 14 MAY 1940

Throughout the morning of 14 May, 50kg and 250kg bombs were loaded aboard the 90 operational Heinkel He 111s of KG 54 at Quakenbruck, Vechta, and Varrelbusch Airfields in western Germany for the scheduled early-afternoon bombardment of Rotterdam. It was decided that the Geschwader would be divided into two forces: Geschwaderkommodore Oberst Walter Lackner, leading the 54 bombers of Stab., II. and III./KG 54 would approach from the east, while Oberstleutnant Otto Höhne would lead the 36 bombers of I./KG 54 from the southwest. The two formations would form an attack triangle with the Nieuwe Maas as its base, and the Nationale Levensverzekering Bank building at the northern end of the road bridge (where the last Fallschirmjäger on the northern side of the Nieuwe Maas were hunkered down) as the centre of the triangle base; the apex of the triangle, where the bombing runs would intersect, would be the Delftse Poort railway station in the centre of the city. The bombardment plan was to isolate Dutch positions along the northern bank of the Nieuwe Maas by creating a swath of destruction that would prevent the defenders from being easily reinforced, while at the same time obstructing their line of withdrawal prior to Schmidt and Student's ground assault. This was hardly the precision attack against individual Dutch positions along the Nieuwe Maas initially envisioned by Student but Göring personally ordered the expanding of the bombardment area.

In addition to supporting the ground assault across the Nieuwe Maas, Göring wanted a show of brute aerial strength, along with threats of further urban bombardments, in an attempt to compel the Dutch to surrender. After taking off from its bases beginning at 1145hrs, KG 54 approached Rotterdam at an altitude of 4,500m. After Höhne broke away with I./KG 54 to approach from the south, Lackner's force encountered heavy cloud cover and had to descend to 750m; most of this cover was smoke, coming from burning ships and oil tanks along the Nieuwe Maas. At 1325hrs Lackner's formation dropped their bombs along their eastward attack angle. Shortly afterwards as I./KG 54 approached from the south, Höhne observed red flares being fired from Noordereiland, the signal to abort the bombardment. The aircraft of Höhne's Stabskette had already dropped their bombs but Höhne immediately radioed the abort order to I./KG 54. German sources claim that the rest of Höhne's formation aborted and did not drop their bombs. Dutch sources suggest that I./KG 54's response to the abort order was more confused. Some bombers were observed breaking formation and some made a wide arc around the city and returned over the target area.

The wide area of destruction along the southern attack angle suggests that more bombs were dropped than those from just three aircraft; furthermore, the detonation pattern of the bombs was more erratic than along the eastern angle. Whatever the reality of the situation was, over one square mile of central Rotterdam was destroyed by the bombardment or consumed in the ensuing fire which burned for a further two days. At least 800 civilians were killed and more than 85,000 were made homeless.

Schmidt and Student wanted to limit the damage on the northern side of the Maas so that northward progress of Schmidt's panzers towards Den Haag and Amsterdam would not be hampered by clogging Rotterdam's narrow streets with debris and wounded civilians. Kesselring responded that the requested Stuka squadrons were not available. Instead, he temporarily assigned KG 54, equipped with He 111s, to Putzier's command for the Rotterdam ground-attack mission. This unit had been involved in attacks across western Belgium and northern France for the last four days. Both Schmidt and Student objected to the use of conventional bombers for this strike but Kesselring insisted, assuring them that KG 54's aircraft could still carry out reasonably accurate attacks. He sent a liaison officer from KG 54 to Schmidt's headquarters that night to go over the precise targets the corps commander wanted hit.

Although Kesselring's precise reasons for refusing use of the Stuka squadrons are not known, it would be reasonable to assume that he was under pressure from Göring to launch a brutal attack on the Dutch with conventional bombers. Göring was well aware that Hitler wanted Dutch resistance brought to an immediate end. This was spelled out in Hitler's *Weisung Nummer 11*, issued on the morning of 14 May, which stated the following regarding operations in the Netherlands: 'On the north wing, the resistance of the Dutch army has proven to be stronger than was assumed. Political and military reasons require that this resistance be broken shortly. The task of the army is to bring the fortress of Holland to

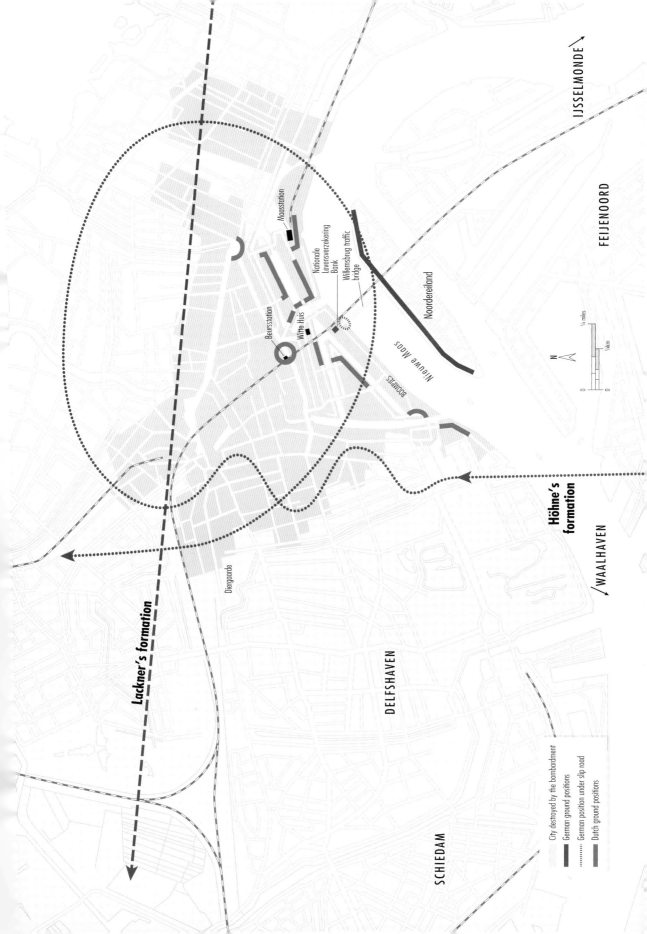

IJSSELMONDE

FEIJENOORD

Maasstation

Nationale
Levensverzekering
Bank

Willemsbrug traffic
bridge

Noordereiland

Beursstation

Witte Huis

Nieuwe Maas

BOOMPJES

N

Höhne's
formation

WAALHAVEN

Lackner's formation

Diergaarde

DELFSHAVEN

SCHIEDAM

0   ¼ miles
0   ¼ km

City destroyed by the bombardment

German ground positions

German position under slip road

Dutch ground positions

collapse quickly with sufficient forces from the south in connection with the attack on the eastern front… The tanks and motorized divisions of the Heeresgruppe B must, as soon as there is no longer any possibility of operative action there and the situation permits, cleared and sent to the left attacking wing.' At 2050hrs, the aerial attack plan for KG 54 was finalized. If the Dutch forces in Rotterdam did not surrender upon the threat of aerial bombardment, the city would be bombed.

The Commando Luchtverdediging was unaware of the German debates and plans for an attack on Rotterdam taking place throughout the night of 13–14 May. On the evening of 13 May, Buiksloot was abandoned by the ML due to a fear (later discovered to be unfounded) that the Germans were preparing to launch an offensive over the Afsluitdijk and river into Noord Holland; Bergen was likewise abandoned in the early hours of 14 May for the same reason. The Combined JaVA, 4ᵉ JaVA were relocated to Schiphol while the StratVerVA was temporarily sent to Ruigenhoek, until the auxiliary airfield at Vogelenzang, just to the north, could be made ready to accommodate it. Like the ground forces of the Koninklijke Leger, the ML planned to fight for the final defence of the Vesting Holland. On the morning of 14 May, the C.-Lvd.'s attention was focused to the east, where the Koninklijke Leger was completing its withdrawal from the Grebbelinie to the Waterlinie. Earlier that night, Baron van Voorst tot Voorst Jr.'s staff requested ML fighter cover beginning at dawn to protect the Dutch columns moving towards the Waterlinie. At 0200hrs, the Combined JaVA and 4ᵉ JaVA were ordered to send up all available fighters at 0400hrs and patrol over the area around Utrecht, keeping the skies over the withdrawing Dutch columns clear of enemy aircraft. Given the weight of German air superiority, this was a formidable order but the Waterlinie was the last line of defence and the backs of the Dutch were against the wall.

Take-off from Schiphol at 0400hrs was impossible due to heavy fog but at 0700hrs the fog was lifting and five D.XXIs and four G.1s were able to begin their mission; D.XXI 221 (Lt. van Overvest), 236 (Lt. Sitter), 242 (Sgt. de Geus), and 244 (Sgt. Hatcboer), led by Lt. Tuininga in 240, with G.1A 322 (Sgt. Hartkoren), G.1B 342 (Lt. Droste), and G.1B 343 (Lt. Steen), led by Lt. van Oorschot in G.1A 308. This mission was unique in that it was the first combat mission undertaken by G.1Bs in ML service, having finally been made combat-ready by Fokker and ML technicians at Schiphol. No enemy aircraft were spotted on this flight, nor were enemy ground troops due to ground fog. The fighters did experience ground fire from nervous Dutch troops on the ground, damaging 236 to the extent that Lt. Sitter had to make an emergency landing just west of Utrecht; the rest of the group returned to Schiphol at 0744hrs. At 1015hrs, the C.-Lvd. decided to send up another fighter patrol over the Utrecht area and, at 1045hrs, five D.XXIs from the Combined JaVA took off: D.XXI 212 (Lt. van de Vaart), 221 (Lt. van der Stok), 224 (Lt. Bik), and 235 (Lt. Plesman), led by Lt. Sluyter in 219. Again, no enemy aircraft or pursuing ground units were encountered and all of the fighters returned to base at 1123hrs. The lack of enemy aerial activity was curious.

At 1115hrs, the C.-Lvd. phoned Ruigenhoek, ordering StratVerVA to undertake an immediate reconnaissance of the German units assembling along the southern end of the Nieuwe Maas around Rotterdam. Between 1200 and 1215hrs, C.Xs 700 and 706 took off and made their way towards Rotterdam employing HU-BO-BE manoeuvres. With ground observation difficult from such a low altitude, C.X 700 climbed to get a better view but in doing so was spotted by roving German fighters. 700 dropped to the deck and escaped to the southwest, eventually making its way to an airfield near Calais in France. C.X 706 made a successful reconnaissance of the area around Rotterdam, although it sustained heavy damage from German ground fire. Much to the surprise of Generals Schmidt and Student, 706 passed low over their headquarters at Rijsoord, southeast of Rotterdam; German anti-aircraft gunners there were so shocked by such a brazen appearance by a Dutch aircraft that they neglected to open fire. Sergeant R.M. van Luijk, 706's pilot, brought his damaged aircraft in for a landing at Ruigenhoek at 1330hrs. Little did van Luijk know that he had just made the ML's last operational sortie of the Meidagen.

At the same time van Luijk touched down at Ruigenhoek, the drone of the 90 He 111s of KG 54 began to be heard over Rotterdam. General Schmidt had scheduled the German assault across the Nieuwe Maas to begin at 1350hrs, to be preceded by an artillery bombardment at 1300 and KG 54's aerial bombardment at 1320. At 0900hrs, he had sent a team of negotiators across the river with a surrender ultimatum to deliver to Kolonel Scharoo. Negotiations between the two parties began and Schmidt was optimistic enough about a possible Dutch surrender that he radioed Putzier at 1230hrs, requesting that KG 54's strike be postponed. Putzier responded that the bombers were already airborne and on their way to the target but that the abort message would be sent. For reasons which are still unclear, it proved impossible to contact the aircraft with the recall order via radio. As the Dutch negotiator was leaving Schmidt's headquarters with his final surrender demands, KG 54's bombers began dropping their payloads over the city. The Germans on the ground fired flares, a pre-arranged signal to the bombers to abort their mission, but only part of the attack force aborted. As Rotterdam burned, Scharoo requested a ceasefire at 1500hrs and went to meet with General Schmidt at 1550. Half an hour later, he signed the surrender of the Dutch forces under his command in Rotterdam.

While Scharoo met with Schmidt, reports reached the Dutch high command that Luftwaffe aircraft were dropping pamphlets over Utrecht, stating that if the Dutch armed forces did not surrender within the next two hours, Utrecht would receive the same aerial bombardment as Rotterdam. Unbeknownst to the Dutch high command, Rotterdam narrowly avoided a second bombardment. Göring had ordered another attack on the city, allegedly to open up a path for Schmidt's panzers to Gen. von Sponeck's forces at Overschie. KG 54's He 111s took off at 1600hrs – the same time that the Dutch had surrendered the city. Upon learning of the incoming raid, Schmidt hurriedly radioed Kesselring to abort the mission. Almost half an hour later, the roar of incoming aircraft was again heard approaching the city but at 1743hrs the planes veered off. At 1650hrs, unwilling to risk further civilian lives in an increasingly one-sided fight, Opperbevelhebber van Land- en Zeemacht Winkelman communicated to Schmidt his intention to surrender and that the Dutch armed forces would lay down their weapons at 1900hrs.

ANALYSIS AND CONCLUSION

In the late summer of 1942, German Fallschirmjäger again descended around the bridges at Moerdijk. This time however they were being recorded by movie cameras for a propaganda film titled *Sprung in den Feind*, or 'Jump into the Enemy', embellishing the success of the Luftwaffe's seemingly invincible sky-warriors against the Dutch defenders at Moerdijk in May 1940. While this film and German media reports from May 1940, as well as many subsequent and even present popular histories of the World War II, gave the impression of an easy victory over the Dutch by Göring's Luftwaffe, they concealed that Unternehmen F could be considered, at best, a limited strategic success whilst a tactical failure. It was a limited strategic success in that Student's Fallschirmjäger and Luftlande troopers, who deployed along the Moerdijk-Rotterdam front, did secure the southern approach into the Vesting Holland just long enough for the arrival of the 9.Panzer-Division. Furthermore, as a result of the bombing of Rotterdam and the threat of further terror bombings, the Netherlands surrendered on the fifth day of the campaign – on this basis, the Luftwaffe claimed victory.

Comparing the lofty goals of Unternehmen F with the losses sustained during the campaign, it is difficult to view it as a successful operation. Of the 3,500 Falschirmjäger and Luftlande troops deployed around Den Haag, 2,735 were killed, wounded, or captured, with roughly 1,350 POWs sent to Great Britain prior to the Dutch surrender. Recent scholarship in the Netherlands and examination of recorded German aircraft crash-landing sites have found that of Luftflotte 2's operational aircraft deployed over the Netherlands for the five days of the campaign, 454 were lost or forced down over Dutch territory: 47 Bf 109s, 14 Bf 110s, 40 He 111s, 7 Ju 87s, 28 Ju 88s, 9 Do 17s, 4 Do 215s, 6 He 59s, 3 He 115s, 2 Hs 123s, 10 Hs 126s, and 284 Ju 52/3ms. When one counts the number of Luftwaffe aircraft which were unserviceable or written off after their return to Germany, the total number of Luftwaffe aircraft put out of action during the Meidagen was around 540. These losses constitute 54 per cent of the aircraft under Kesselring's command during the campaign. Although a number of these aircraft were salvageable and some were returned to service, this was a devastating loss rate for the Luftwaffe against the first integrated air-defence system it encountered during the war. This did not bode well for the Luftwaffe's impending clash with the RAF in the Battle of Britain.

The losses of fighters and bombers in Unternehmen F did not impede the overall progress of Fall Gelb but the losses of transport aircraft had strategic consequences. Of the 455 aircraft put out of service, 284 were Ju 52/3ms, or 69 per cent of those deployed in the campaign. As a result, Hitler insisted during the planning for *Unternehmen Seelöwe* (Operation *Sealion*) – the planned invasion of Great Britain – that air supremacy must be achieved by the Luftwaffe over south-west England before any airborne operations could be attempted – something the Luftwaffe would prove unable to achieve. Kesselring and the staff of Luftflotte 2 acknowledged after the war that the transport losses in the Netherlands, when also factoring in the losses of experienced air crews, limited the Luftwaffe's airborne capabilities for the remainder of the war. Although the level of losses was covered up, the Luftwaffe arguably never recovered.

Finally, unlike Hitler and Kesselring, Göring walked away from Unternehmen F with his hubris intact. Sweeping the débâcle at Den Haag under the carpet, he boasted that his bombers had, at Rotterdam, brought about the Dutch surrender. This myth that terror bombing alone could achieve a strategic campaign objective would send many Luftwaffe bomber pilots to their graves during the Blitz over London.

For the Dutch, the Meidagen campaign resulted in exceptionally high aircraft losses for the ML. On 10 May alone, it lost 17 Fokker D.XXIs, 17 G.IAs, 12 T.Vs, 7 C.Xs, 18 C.Vs, 14 Douglas DB 8As, 17 Koolhoven FK-51s, and 19 training and liaison aircraft. Over the next four days, up until the bombardment of Rotterdam, it lost an additional 3 D.XXIs, 5 G.1As, 6 D.XVIIs, 2 T.Vs, 17 C.Vs, 4 FK 51s, and 7 other aircraft. A total of 165 aircraft had been lost in combat or due to Luftwaffe strafing missions and ground attacks. When Opperbevelhebber van Land- en Zeemacht Winkelman went on the radio and announced

German soldiers watching Rotterdam burn, following KG 54's bombardment of the city centre on the afternoon of 14 May. (Getty Images)

The Meidagen was not the final campaign for a number of ML pilots. Several made their way, along with other Dutch volunteers, to Great Britain and went on to serve in the Royal Air Force. Photographed here in 1945 is Squadron Leader Bram van der Stok (centre with back to the map), formerly of 1e JaVA, as the commander of No. 322 (Dutch) Squadron RAF. The pilot to the left of the one in the white sweater is Jan Linzel, formerly of the 1e Afdeling van de Jachtgroep Veldleger. (Collectie Nederlands Instituut voor Militaire Historie)

to the Dutch population the surrender of the armed forces that remained in the Netherlands at 1900hrs on 14 May, the squadrons of the ML were ordered to destroy their records and their remaining aircraft. Over the course of the evening, ML crews destroyed 11 D.XXIs, 5 G.IAs, 2 G.IBs, 1 D.XVIIs, 7 C.Xs, 8 C.Vs, and 10 other training aircraft. Given the amount of wear and tear and battle damage sustained by the ML's squadrons over five days of intense combat, it is surprising that this many aircraft were still operational on the evening of 14 May. These remaining aircraft were hardly in pristine order either. Routine maintenance procedures could rarely be completed between missions and there had been instances of pilots taking up their aircraft without canopies, with leaking brake systems, and holed wings and fuselages.

The willingness of the ML's pilots to continue to fly in these circumstances demonstrated their determination to take the fight to the enemy, regardless of the odds. Most wanted to continue the fight against the Germans, despite the surrender. Several KLM aircraft had been made operational at Schiphol and a number of ML air crews wanted to depart for Great Britain to fight under Queen Wilhelmina and the Free Dutch forces that would eventually be assembled there. However, the ML leadership instructed its pilots and crews not to leave the country, stating that the conditions of the ceasefire with the Germans required Dutch military personnel to remain in the Netherlands. Liutenants Van der Stok and Jan Plesman would later escape to Great Britain where they, and other countrymen who escaped the occupied Netherlands, would join the Dutch RAF No. 322 Squadron, flying Spitfire fighters against the Luftwaffe; van der Stok eventually became No 322's commanding officer in March 1945. Despite the heavy aircraft losses and the brevity of the campaign, the ML fought a hard fight and achieved the seemingly impossible – it delivered the Luftwaffe its first significant setback in World War II.

BIBLIOGRAPHY

Primary sources

ML Pilot Accounts and Post-war Reports of the Commando Luchtverdediging, located in the collections of the Netherlands Institute of Military History (NIMH)

Secondary sources

Ausems, Andre. 'The Netherlands Military Intelligence Summaries 1939–1940 and the Defeat in the Blitzkrieg of May 1940.' *Military Affairs* 50, no. 4 (1986): 190–199.

Beekman, Frans S.A. *Sturmangriff aus der Luft.* Berg am See: Vowinckel, 1990.

Bekker, Cajus. *Angriffshöhe 4000: Die deutsche Luftwaffe im Zweiten Weltkrieg.* München: Wilhelm Heyne Verlag, 1968.

Bosscher, Ph.M. *De Koninklijke Marine in de Tweede Wereldoorlog.* 3 Volumes. Franeker: Uitgeverij T. Wever B.V., 1984.

Brongers, Lt. Col. E.H. *The Battle for The Hague.* Soesterberg: Uitgeverij Aspekt, 2004.

-----. 'Inventarisatie uit diverse bronnen van in de Meidagen van 1940 tijdens of door de strijd in Nederland neergeschoten, vernielde of door vuur beschadigde duitse vliegtuigen, weergegeven per provincie of gebied.' Unpublished manuscript, 2008. https://www.grebbeberg.nl/uploads/downloads/brongers_verlies_duitse_vltgn_mei40.pdf

-----. *Opmars naar Rotterdam, Deel I.* Soesterberg: Uitgeverij Aspekt, 2004.

Bruin, Rob de, et al. *Illusies en Incidenten: De Militaire Luchtvaart en de neutraliteitshandhaving to 10 mei 1940.* 's-Gravenhage: Koninklijke Luchtmacht / Bureau Drukwerk en Formulierenbeheer DMKLu, 1988.

Caldwell, Donald L. *JG 26: Top Guns of the Luftwaffe.* New York: Orion Books, 1991.

Cornwell, Peter D. *The Battle of France: Then and Now.* Old Harlow: Battle of Britain International Ltd., 2007.

Edwards, Roger. *German Airborne Troops 1936–45.* Garden City: Doubleday & Company, 1974.

Gerdessen, Frits and Luuk Boerman. *Fokker D.XXI: historie, camouflage en kentekens.* Zwammerdam: Dutch Profile, 2007.

Götzel, Hermann and Kurt Student. *Generaloberst Kurt Student und seine Fallschirmjäger: die Erinnerungen des Generaloberst Kurt Student.* Friedberg: Podzun-Pallas-Verlag, 1980.

Grimm, Peter, et al. *Verliesregister 1939–1945 Alle militaire vliegtuigverliezen in Nederland tijdens de Tweede Wereldoorlog.* Den Haag: Studiegroep Luchtoorlog 1939–1945, 2008.

Gundelach, Karl. *Kamfgeschwader 'General Wever' 4: Eine Geschichte aus Kriegstagebüchern, Dokumenten und Berichten 1939–1945.* Stuttgart: Motorbuch Verlag, 1978.

Hartog, L.J. 'Het bombardement van Rotterdam op 14 mei 1940.' *De Gids: Algemeen Cultureel Maandblad.* Jaargang 122 (1959): pp. 227–50.

Helfferich, Willem. *Squadrons van de Koninklijke Luchtmacht.* Rotterdam: Drukkerij Wyt & Zn., 1994.

Hooten, E.R. *Phoenix Triumphant: The Rise and Rise of the Luftwaffe.* London: Arms & Armour Press, 1994.

Jacobsen, Hans Adolf. 'Der deutsche Luftangriff auf Rotterdam; Versuch einer Klärung.' *Wehrwissenschaftliche Rundschau; Zeitschrift für die europäische Sicherheit*, Vol. VIII, No. 5 (May 1958): pp. 257–84.

-----.*Fall Gelb: der Kampf um den deutschen Operationsplan zur Westoffensive 1940*. Wiesbaden: F. Steiner, 1957.

Jong, L. de. *Het Koninkrijk der Nederlanden in de Tweede Wereldoorlog*. Deel I–III. 's-Gravenhage: Staatsuitgeverij, 1969.

Kesselring, Albert. *Soldat bis zum letzten Tag*. Bonn: Athenäum-Verlag, 1953.

Kruk, Marek and Radosław Szewczyk. *9th Panzer Division 1940–1943*. Petersfield: Mushroom Model Publications, 2011.

Loo, P.E. van. '"Eenige wakkere jongens": Nederlandse oorlogsvliegers in de Britse luchtstrijdkrachten 1940–1945.' Ph.D Thesis, University of Amsterdam, 2013.

Maier, Klaus A., et al. *Germany and the Second World War. Volume II, Germany's Initial Conquests in Europe*. Oxford: Oxford University Press, 1991.

Mallan, K. Mallan. *Als de Dag van Gistern… De Duitse Overrompeling en Vernietiging van Nederlands Eerste Havenstad. Weesp*: De Gooise Uitgeverij, 1985.

Molenaar, F.J. *De luchtverdediging in de meidagen 1940*. twee banden. Den Haag: Staatsuitgeverij, 1970.

Morzik, Generalmajor a.D. Fritz. German Air Force Airlift Operations. Maxwell AFB: USAF Historical Division, Research Studies Institute, Air University, 1961.

Mosier, John. *The Blitzkrieg Myth: How Hitler and the Allies Misread the Strategic Realities of World War II*. New York: HarperCollins, 2003.

Paterson, Lawrence. *Eagles Over the Sea 1935–1942: A History of Luftwaffe Maritime Operations*. Barnsley: Seaforth Publishing, 2019.

Pauw, J.L. van der. *Rotterdam in de Tweede Wereldoorlog*. Rotterdam: Uitgeverij Boom, 2006.

Pearson, Frederic S. *The Weak State in International Crisis: The Case of the Netherlands in the German Invasion Crisis of 1939–40*. Washington D.C.: University Press of America, 1981.

Postma, S.J. *HU-BO-BE: De strategische VerVa in de oorlogsdagen van 1940*. Assen: Born's Uitgeversbedrijf N.V., 1945.

Quarrie, Bruce. *German Airborne Divisions: Blitzkrieg 1940–41*. Oxford: Osprey Publishing, 2004.

Schoenmaker, Wim and Thijs Postma. *KLu Vliegtuigen*. Alkmaar: Uitgeverij De Alk, 1987.

Schuurman, J.H. *Vliegveld Bergen NH 1938–1945*. Bergen: Uitgeverij De Coogh, 2001.

Speidel, Wilhelm. *The German Air Force in France and the Low Countries 1939–1940, Volume 3*. Karlsruhe: Studiengruppe Geschichte des Luftkrieges, 1958.

Smith, J.R. and A.L. Kay. *German Aircraft of the Second World War*. London: Putnam Aeronautical Books, 1972.

Starink, D. 'De jonge jaren van de luchtmacht: Het luchtwapen in het Nederlandse leger 1913–1939.' PhD diss., Amsterdam Institute for Humanities Research, 2013.

Steenbeek, Wilhelmina. *Rotterdam: Invasion of Holland*. New York: Ballantine, 1973.

Weiss, Heinrich. 'Luftkrieg über Holland 10–15 Mai.' Segments of unpublished manuscript. Douglas Dildy Collection.

Wesselink, Theo and Thijs Postma. *Koolhoven: Nederlands vliegtuigbouwer in de schaduw van Fokker*. Haarlem: Romen, 1981.

Whiting, Charles. *Hunters from the Sky: The German Parachute Corps 1940–1945*. London: Leo Cooper, 1974.

INDEX